Life
and
Building

as Portrayed
in the
Song
of Songs

Witness Lee

Living Stream Ministry
Anaheim, CA • www.lsm.org

First Edition, December 1979.

ISBN 978-0-87083-024-2

Published by

Living Stream Ministry
2431 W. La Palma Ave., Anaheim, CA 92801 U.S.A.
P. O. Box 2121, Anaheim, CA 92814 U.S.A.

Printed and bound by CPI Group (UK) Ltd, Croydon, CR0 4YY
14   15   16   17   18   19   /   14   13   12   11   10   9

CONTENTS

The Scripture references used in this book are taken from various translations which give the best rendering of the text.

PREFACE

This book is composed of messages given by Brother Witness Lee in Los Angeles, California, from April 18 through June 7, 1972.

Chapter One

WHAT IS LIFE?

Scripture Reading: Gen. 2:9-12; John 14:6a; 1 John 5:12; Col. 3:4a; Gal. 2:20a; Rev. 21:2, 18-19a, 21; 22:1-2a

By reading the above verses, we can see life and building. Many of us have been Christians for years and may have heard about life, but may have never heard anything about building. Life is for building. Life is the content, and building is the corporate expression of this content. So if we have life, normally speaking, we should have building; and if we would have building, we must have life. God purposes to express Himself through a corporate Body. Therefore, God must be life to a group of people who must be built up to express God in a corporate way.

THE BASIC REVELATION OF THE BIBLE

Life is just God Himself, and building is simply the expression of God as life in a corporate Body. Life and building are the basic and central revelation of the Bible. Genesis 2 shows that after God completed His creation, especially the creation of man, He put man into a garden in which the central item was the tree of life. Here we must underline the word *life*. As it is very difficult to define life, so it is also difficult to define the tree of life. You know what a peach tree is and what an apple tree is, but you may not know what the tree of life is. From other books in the Bible, we can realize that this tree of life is nothing less than God Himself. The Triune God is the tree of life to us.

Then we see some precious things that come out of the flow of this life. Near the tree of life is a flowing river, and at the flow of the river there is gold, bdellium (a kind of pearl), and onyx stone (Gen. 2:9-12). Life produces the flow of life, and out of the flow of life come these three kinds of precious materials: gold, pearl, and precious stone. To know what these are for, we must read the Bible through to the end where we see a city that is built with gold, pearl, and precious stones (Rev. 21:2, 18-19a, 21; 22:1-2a). Therefore, these three precious materials indicate building.

So, we see that the Bible opens with life for the building. Life is the source, and the building is the issue of life. Many Christians know that the Bible is a book of life, but not many Christians realize life in a proper and adequate way. We need to see some of the wrong views that Christians have concerning life. However, from these verses in Genesis and Revelation, we can see clearly that life is for building and that building comes out of life.

LIFE BEING DIFFERENT FROM KNOWLEDGE

Life has nothing to do with knowledge. Instead, knowledge is versus life. In Genesis 2:9 there are two trees: the tree of life and the tree of the knowledge of good and evil. By this picture we can understand that knowledge is contrary to life and even versus life. Why must I mention this? Simply because in any kind of religion, and especially in Christianity, people always pay attention to knowledge. After we were saved in Christianity, we were told to give attention to knowledge. Yet the Bible shows us that knowledge is contrary to life and versus life. If we are going to know what life is and realize the experience of life, we must first of all be very clear concerning the difference between life and knowledge.

For example, if you drink a glass of milk, you get life. If you do not drink it, regardless of how much you know about it, you have mere knowledge. To know about milk is just knowledge, but to take it into you is nourishment, and that is life. Life is not knowledge, and knowledge can never replace life. Instead, knowledge contradicts life.

If we would care for life, we must, in a sense, repudiate knowledge. We should not care for knowledge. We should only care for taking something into us to nourish us. Knowledge will bring us death instead of life. Furthermore, knowledge causes not only death but also division. If knowledge is the main emphasis among us, I fear that after a short time we will be divided into several sects. So we must take off the crown of knowledge and put it under our feet—then we will have one-ness. Knowledge divides, but life unites.

LIFE BEING DIFFERENT FROM GIFTS

Because spiritual gifts are mentioned in the Bible, Chris-tians may have the misunderstanding that gifts are something of life. But gifts are different from life. Genesis 2:9 proves strongly that knowledge is contrary to life, and 1 Corinthians proves that gifts are not life.

First Corinthians 1:7 points out that the Corinthian believers did not lack in any gift. The context of this verse reveals that they had all the gifts and all knowledge and utterance. We would think that surely they must be full of life. But we must read the first four verses of 1 Corinthians 3: "I, brothers, was not able to speak to you as to spiritual men, but as to fleshy, as to infants in Christ. I gave you milk to drink, not solid food, for you were not yet able to receive it. But neither yet now are you able, for you are still fleshly. For if there is jealousy and strife among you, are you not fleshly and do you not walk according to the manner of man? For when someone says, I am of Paul, and another, I of Apollos, are you not men of flesh?" Paul told them that they were not spiritual but fleshly and babyish. He could not feed them with solid food but with milk because of their condition. They had all the gifts, yet they were still infants in Christ. This proves strongly that you may have the gifts and yet not have much life.

Many times I have used the illustration of Balaam's don-key in the Old Testament. A Gentile prophet by the name of Balaam had a donkey that suddenly spoke in a human lan-guage (Num. 22:28-30). For a donkey to speak a human language is a real gift of tongues. It was not the result of human manufacture, and it was not artificial or superficial. It was a genuine tongue given by divine power; otherwise, how could a donkey speak with the human language? But did that donkey receive the human life? It received the gift to function but not the life. No matter how much it spoke the human language, it was not a human; it was still a donkey. A donkey is still a donkey, even though it may speak the human language better than I do. I am a human being, and it is not; I do not have its gift, but I have the human life. It has the gift but not the human life.

To know life, we must clearly discern the difference between life and knowledge and between life and gifts. Do you still consider gifts as life? Suppose we have a person who speaks in tongues often and another person who has a powerful healing gift. Do you consider these gifts as life? If you do, you misunderstand life. Life is different from knowledge, and life is different from gifts.

LIFE BEING DIFFERENT FROM POWER

We must also see that life also differs from power. Electricity is a kind of power; we even call it electrical power. But there is no life in that power. Thus, we may be powerful and still be short of life. We can see this especially in one person in the Old Testament. Samson was very powerful, yet he was short of life (Judg. 16). We can never take him as an example of life. He might be an example of power, but he was short of life.

Many Christians today also have this misunderstanding—they think that if you have power, surely you must have life. But power is power, and life is life. You may be exceedingly powerful and still not have much life. The Lord Jesus said in Luke 24:49, "Behold, I send forth the promise of My Father upon you; but as for you, stay in the city until you put on power from on high." The Lord told the disciples to wait until they put on power, which He likened to an article of clothing. We all know that an article of clothing does not have life. If a policeman were to take off his uniform, he would lose his power, but he would still be living. This power is not related to life. If you were driving a car, and a policeman signaled you to stop, you would stop immediately. This is because he exercises power. But that power is not life.

We must be clear that life is different from knowledge, gifts, and power. Today in Christianity there is a very serious trend. Many Christians give their attention either to knowledge, gifts, or power, but very few give their full attention to life. Can we find any power or gifts in Genesis 2? We can only find knowledge mentioned in a negative way, and there is no mention of gifts or power. Can we find them in Revelation 21 and 22? All we see in that holy city is life, life, life! There is the tree of life and the river of water of life. Only life is for eternity.

We must come back to the pure Word in the Lord's recovery. The Lord's recovery brings us back to the beginning. We must tell others that the Bible shows us in Genesis 2 and Revelation 21 and 22 that life is the main emphasis. According to the Bible, we can clearly see that life is different from knowledge, gifts, and power.

LIFE BEING A PERSON

Then what is life? Life is God Himself. Life is Jesus! In John 11:25 and 14:6 Jesus said, "I am...the life." Colossians 3:4 speaks of "Christ our life." Life is a wonderful person!

Simply to say that life is a person is quite easy, but it takes time for us to get into the experience. The very life that we received when we believed in the Lord Jesus is a person! Do you know the difference between a person and a life? With a person there is a personality with a will, desires, intentions, and emotions. But a life may not have all these aspects. A tree has life, but this life has no personality, no will, no intention, and no desire. But the life that we have received of the Lord Jesus is not a mere life; it is a person! It is a person with a divine and a human personality. This person has a will, an intention, and a desire. This is the life that we have received of the Lord.

THREE KINDS OF LIVES

According to the Greek New Testament, there are three different kinds of lives: the bios (physical) life, the psuche (psychological) life, and the zoe (eternal) life. We must realize that the zoe life is not merely a life; it is a divine-human person. The Lord Jesus is the unique person with both the divine personality and the human personality. The zoe life

that you received when you were saved is a person. Hallelujah!

THE STRONGEST PERSON

But with such a person there is a problem. If zoe was
merely a life, it would be easy to deal with it. But since the
zoe life is a person, we have some problems. Simply to take
life is easy, but to take a person is not so easy. If I were just a
mere life, it would be easy for you to deal with me. But in fact
it is really difficult for you to deal with me because I am a
person.

The main problem between husbands and wives is that
they are persons with different personalities. A man has a
male personality, and a woman has a female personality.
When two personalities are put together, there really is a
problem. If all the brothers' wives had no personality, it
would be wonderful! But the problem is that each of our wives
has a unique, strong personality. And the brothers' personalities are just as unique and strong. The problem always
arises from the matter of personality. This is why life is a
problem.

The Lord Jesus, who is our life, is a person. If we do not
take Him as a person, then we do not have life. If we take life,
we must take Him as a person. First John 5:12 says, "He who
has the Son has the life; and he who does not have the Son of
God does not have the life." The Son is a person. This verse
does not say that he who has the life of the Son has life. It
says that he who has the Son has life! The person is the life.
If we do not take this person, it will be rather difficult for us
to get the life. The life is the person! If this vision could be
wrought into us, it would be wonderful. We all must be clear
that the zoe life is a person.

Moreover, Christ is a person with the strongest personality! We can be assured that His personality is much stronger
than ours, and that it can never be subdued by ours. He is
waiting continually to subdue our personality with His.

Zoe is not merely a life without a personality but a person
as life. If we take zoe as our life, then surely we must take
Jesus as our person, because this life is a person.

THE BASIC NEED

We do praise the Lord that many have been turned to the Lord and attracted to the church life. This is really wonderful. Several are also having many outward changes, and this too is wonderful. Our basic need, however, is not just an outward turn but a turn within that we may see what God desires. It is not what we are but what Christ is within us. We must learn by the help of the Lord to repudiate and hate ourselves. Regardless of whether our self is good or bad, we must hate the self, because it is an enemy and adversary to Christ. We not only have the outward enemy but also the inward adversary to Christ. So we must say to the Lord, "Lord, I hate myself. Whatever I do, whatever I am, whatever I speak is hateful. I hate what I do, I hate what I am, and I hate what I speak. I hate it because it is an enemy to You."

We all need such a basic turn so that Christ can become our life. It is not just an outward turn but an inward turn. It is not sufficient to turn from Babylon to the church. This is wonderful, and I praise the Lord for it. It is good to turn from Babylon to Jerusalem, but this is still just an outward turn. We all need a deeper, inward turn within to realize that Christ, as a person, is our life. We not only have another life but also another person. Jesus, the unique person, the divine and human person, is now our life. To take Him as our life, we must take Him as a whole person. This is why Paul says, "I am crucified with Christ; and it is no longer I who live, but it is Christ who lives in me" (Gal. 2:20). It is no longer I, but it is Christ. I was the old person, and now Christ is the new person. The old person has been nullified, crossed out on the cross. Now it is the new person, Christ, who is living in me. Paul does not say that it is the life of Christ that lives in me. No, he says that it is no longer I, but *Christ* who lives in me. It is no longer the old person but now a new person who is wonderful and unique. This new person is divine as well as human, and this unique, strong person lives in me as my life. Oh, may the Lord open our eyes! We must go to the Lord and say, "Lord, show me something deeper; show me something higher so that I may have such a basic inward turn."

Many times I have seen things in the churches that were not so good. Yet I never dared to correct or regulate, because I realized that outward correction and regulation mean nothing. The most precious thing is an inward turn. We must forget our old person, who is our self, and turn to our new person, who is Christ. If we take this new person as our life, we will see the result. There will be the flow of life. To take Christ as our life releases the flow of life. Later on we will see that by this flow of life comes transformation. Pieces of clay are transformed into precious stones. But this is not by any outward doing. I thank God for our turn from Babylon to Jerusalem, yet we all need a basic inward turn from our old person to the new person. This is life. Life is not knowledge, it is not gifts, neither is it power. Life is a wonderful, unique, and strong person.

A PERSONAL CONTACT

Since this life is such a person, we must contact Him. He is not a teaching to learn, and He is not some kind of faith to believe in. Life is a living person to contact and deal with. If I am staying with a certain brother, I must continually contact him as a living person. If he is away, I still must call him frequently; otherwise, I cannot say that I know this brother very well. I may have considerable knowledge about him, but how much I know means nothing. To really know him as a person, I must contact him all the time. I cannot say that, because I have known him for twenty years, I have no need to contact him now. If so, I will miss his presence. I constantly need a personal contact with him.

Since Jesus as our life is a person, we must contact Him. Do not tell others that you have known Jesus for twenty years. That means very little. You may have known Jesus for over twenty years and yet today miss His presence. Perhaps I came to know Him just five minutes ago, but I am in His presence. Thus, I get Him, and you miss Him. We must forget about our knowledge and past experiences. We even need to forget all that we know about Jesus. It means little. We need the present presence of Jesus. We need His presence at this very moment and day by day. We need the present person all the time, no matter how much we have known Him and experienced Him in the past. We need a new contact with Christ all day, moment by moment. He is a living person within us, so we must contact Him. We must tell Him, "Lord Jesus, I love You! O Lord Jesus, I love You! I hate and repudiate myself. I put myself aside so that I may take You as my life, moment by moment and day by day."

Thus, we can see that life is not knowledge, gifts, or power. I appreciate these things in their proper place, but I can tell you from my experiences that nothing but life can build up the church. And this life is just Christ as the unique, living person. When we take Him as our life, we are in the process of being built up. Praise the Lord! This is all we need.

CHAPTER TWO

LOVING CHRIST THE PERSON

Scripture Reading: 1 Tim. 1:14; 2 Cor. 5:14-15; Gal. 2:20; John 14:21, 23; 21:15-19; Rev. 2:4

In the first chapter we saw that life is simply Christ Himself. Christ as life to us is a person. We can deal with many things without love, but we cannot deal with a person without love. We may deal with a table or a chair without love, but not with a person.

Suppose I am your roommate. If you do not love me, you will find it very difficult to have me as your roommate. It would be difficult for me to stay with you, and it would be difficult for you to stay with me. So love is needed in order to deal with a living person.

According to the Bible, our relationship to the Lord is likened to a marriage. We are His bride, and He is our Groom. A bride and a groom must have love. If a marriage lacks love, then that marriage will have difficulties. It is impossible to have a genuine marriage without love. Marriage is built uniquely upon love. Without love, there is no marriage life. Likewise, our relationship with the Lord is like a marriage, and this marriage depends upon love. There is no problem on the Lord's side, for He certainly loves us. The problem is on our side. Do we love the Lord Jesus? When someone mentions the name of Jesus, do we have a sweet feeling within? Whenever we think even a little about Him, are we attracted to Him?

FAITH AND LOVE

Paul says in 1 Timothy 1:14, "The grace of our Lord superabounded with faith and love in Christ Jesus." Grace is abundant in two aspects: in faith and in love in Christ Jesus. Originally, Paul as Saul of Tarsus had nothing to do with Jesus Christ. He was even full of hatred toward the Lord. But one day he received mercy and grace from the Lord not only to believe in Jesus but also to love Him. Once, he hated Jesus; then, by the grace of God, he loved Jesus. This is the greatest mercy, and this is real grace. It is not enough just to believe in the Lord Jesus. We also must love Him. I am sure that we have all thanked God for His mercy and grace which have caused us to believe in the Lord Jesus. But have we ever prayed, "O Father, how I thank You that by Your grace I love the Lord Jesus"? Not only do we need faith but also love.

The entire Gospel of John shows us these two things. In the first part of the Gospel, we read that the Lord Jesus, who was God Himself, was the Word in the beginning. Then one day He became incarnated as a man to tabernacle among us, full of grace and reality. John's Gospel encourages us to believe in this One. One of the most important verbs in the Gospel of John is *believe*. The Word became flesh, and we must believe in Him. To believe simply means to receive. John 1:12 says, "As many as received Him, to them He gave the authority to become children of God, to those who believe into His name." We believe by receiving, and we receive by believing. We believe what God has given, and by believing we receive what He gives.

But this is not all. In the Gospel of John, after speaking of believing, the Lord Jesus appealed for our love. He told us, "He who loves Me will be loved by My Father, and I will love him and will manifest Myself to him...If anyone loves Me, he will keep My word, and My Father will love him, and We will come to him and make an abode with him" (14:21, 23). In these verses the Lord Jesus did not say, "He who believes in Me." To believe in the Lord is one thing, but to love Him is another. To believe is to receive, *but to love is to enjoy what you have received.* So in the last chapter of John's Gospel, the Lord asked Peter three times, "Do you love Me?" By this, the Lord was showing Peter that, as one who had received Him, he must learn to enjoy Him by loving Him.

We know that the sisters go to the supermarket, buy many groceries, and store them. Though these groceries are bought and stored, they have not yet been enjoyed. Therefore, the sisters must not only store them but also enjoy them.

It is unnecessary for me to ask if you believe in the Lord Jesus. But I have a big question mark as to whether you love the Lord Jesus. Tell me honestly, do you love the Lord Jesus? Do you love Him more than all other things? Peter could say, "Lord, You know that I love You." Can we say the same thing? With an honest heart, can we say, "Lord Jesus, You know that I love You"? Now that we have believed in the Lord, He is appealing for our love.

Suppose I give a nice Bible to a brother. I want him not only to receive it but to love it and spend much time with it. This is why believing in the Lord is one thing but loving Him is something deeper. Paul said that the grace of our Lord superabounded to him with both the believing and the loving. It is by His grace that we believed in the Lord Jesus, and it is also by His grace that we love the Lord Jesus. We have faith in Him as well as love for Him. We believe in Him, and we love Him.

LOVING JESUS

Have you ever noticed the length of Galatians 2:20? For many years I thought that that verse was too long. "I am crucified with Christ; and it is no longer I who live, but it is Christ who lives in me"—to me, just that much was sufficient. Many times I quoted just the first part of Galatians 2:20, thinking that the last half was unnecessary. But Paul added, "who loved me and gave Himself up for me." Paul simply could not contain himself. Since he had such a One living in him, the love of Christ constrained him. It is a constraining power. The love of Christ constrains us to live no more unto ourselves. He loved me and gave Himself up for me; now I love Him and live by Him.

The apostle Paul had been an enemy and persecutor of the Lord Jesus. But at a certain time the Lord knocked him to the ground. Then he was turned from being an enemy and a persecutor of Jesus to being one who loved Jesus. Real power is in love. Love can do everything. All the mothers know that there are many things that no one but mothers can do for their children, because mothers have the loving power. If we really love the Lord Jesus, we will have the power and strength to do anything for Him.

I once read a poem that was written by a sister near the time of her martyrdom. I cannot quote it, but I can recall the main point. She said that every martyr of Jesus loves Jesus and that everyone who loves Jesus will give his life for Jesus. Can you die for others? If you love them, you can. Love makes this possible. Nothing but love could make us die for others. If we love Jesus, we will be willing to die for Him. This was why the Lord Jesus asked Peter, "Do you love Me?" He asked him three times, and Peter answered, "Lord, You know that I love You." Then eventually the Lord told him how he would die. "Truly, truly, I say to you, When you were younger, you girded yourself and walked where you wished; but when you grow old, you will stretch out your hands, and another will gird you and carry you where you do not wish to go. Now this He said, signifying by what kind of death he would glorify God" (John 21:18-19). As one who loved Jesus, Peter would also be a martyr for Jesus.

Do you think that to follow and sacrifice your life for Jesus is a suffering? On the contrary, it is really an enjoyment because we love Him. The power is in the love.

ENJOY BY LOVING

Life is a person, and there is no other way to apply and enjoy this person but by love. We need to love Him. Some of the saints in past centuries used to pray, "Lord, show me Your love that I may love You." We need to pray the same prayer. Once we see the love of Jesus, we will be so constrained, so captured, and so attracted. We will spontaneously love Him. Then by loving Him, we will enjoy Him. This is life, and since this life is a person, there is no other way for us to experience Him but by love. Only by loving Jesus can we enjoy Him.

If I want to enjoy a brother, I must love that brother. The more I love him, the more I enjoy him. The Lord Jesus is not a doctrine; He is not a set of gifts or a power; He is a person who needs our love, our appreciation, and our affection. How we need the sweet affection and love toward the Lord Jesus!

Many Christians today hold the teachings but are so cold toward the Lord. They have all the doctrines, the dispensations, the prophecies, and the types. Some even have doctor's degrees in divine teachings, yet they are so cold toward the Lord Jesus. We can deal with teachings in this way, but we cannot deal with this person in a cold way. We can exercise our mind to deal with all the doctrines, and yet our heart remains cold. If we are going to deal with this person, we must have a hot and loving heart, a heart so full of affection that we would contact Him all the time. One book among the sixty-six books of the Bible, the Song of Songs, illustrates how the Lord Jesus is altogether lovely. This book shows how the Lord is so attractive and how we are those who love Him. We just love Him! Could you love some doctrine in this way? I do not believe that you could even love the gifts in this way. Do you love the gifts? Could you say, "O dear gifts, you are altogether lovely! Oh, the healing! Oh, the speaking in tongues! All the gifts are so sweet!"? Just try to speak in this way. It simply does not fit. But we can say a thousand times, "Lord Jesus, You are altogether lovely! O Lord Jesus, You are altogether lovely!"

Suppose you have the best furniture in your home. The chairs, the sofas, the desks, and the bedroom furniture are all very beautiful and expensive. But could you love them like you love a person? Could you go to one of the chairs and tell it, "Little chair, I just love you. You are altogether lovely"? Could you do that? I simply could not do it. I do care for all the furniture in my apartment, but I have never told it how much I love it. I simply cannot express myself in this way. But the more you say this to a person, the more there is the sweet love and enjoyment. This is because there is the affectionate attachment in a person. The Lord Jesus is not a chair; He is not a sofa; neither is He a teaching, a doctrine, a gift, or a power. He is a loving person. "My Beloved is altogether lovely! He is my life!" This life is nothing else but a lovely person.

We may talk about Christ being our life, but if we do not have the real love toward Him, He is only life to us in doctrine. We just have the doctrine of Christ as life; we do not have the enjoyment of Him as life. If we would enjoy Jesus as life, we must love Him. As long as we love Him, even if we do not know the term *life,* we will enjoy life. We will not know a doctrine, but we will enjoy Jesus, a living person, as our very life.

TAKING THE LORD'S PERSONALITY

Suppose I tell a certain brother that I love him. This involves a lot. He is a person with a strong personality, having his own will, desires, and intentions. He also has his likes and dislikes. I say that I love him, but does this mean that I ask him to follow my desire? This is not love; this is a demand. If I really love him, I must follow his desire. This is why the Lord told Simon Peter to follow Him after Peter said that he loved Him. The Lord was saying that to take Him as our life and as our person, we must take His desire as our desire. We must take His will as our will. We must take His intention as our intention. To love Him as a person, we must take His personality.

If you are a husband, do you really love your wife? The best way to love your wife is by taking her personality, taking her will as your will. Suppose I am a husband, and I tell my dear wife, "Oh, I love you, but you must realize that I am the head! You have to submit yourself to me! Whatever I say, you must follow me!" Is this love? If I really know what love is, I would take her personality as my personality. I would take her will as my will. I would take her intention as my intention. However, to say this is easy, but to do it requires real love.

With the sisters it is the same. Do not say that because you love your husband, you prepare something for him. You may think that you prove your love in this way, but he may not like what you prepare. Merely to prepare something for him is not love. To love him is to take his desire as your desire and to take his personality as your personality.

We may have many teachings with all the gifts and power, and yet we would not take the personality of Christ. The Lord

Jesus does not need someone who has teachings, gifts, and power. He needs someone like Peter to love Him, someone to tell Him, "O Lord Jesus, I love You! I follow You. I take You as my person. I take Your personality as my personality. I take Your will as my will. I take Your desire as my desire. I do not care for teachings, gifts, and power. I just care for You. I love You, and I follow You, taking You as my person."

During the past years of my Christian life, I have heard many teachings, and I have been taught to do many things. But nothing works unless we love the Lord Jesus. Some people teach that we must reckon ourselves dead with Christ. But if we do not love Him, regardless of how much we reckon ourselves dead, we are never dead. On the other hand, if we say from our heart, "Lord Jesus, I love You; I take Your personality as my personality," there is no need for us to reckon ourselves dead; we are dead already.

Others teach about holiness. But what is holiness? Holiness is simply the Lord Jesus Himself. If we try to be holy and have holiness, we get nothing. But if we just tell the Lord all day long, "Lord Jesus, I love You," something will happen. When we are in the department store, let us say with every item we pick up, "Lord Jesus, I love You." Automatically, so many things will be dropped. Eventually, we will come home with nothing but the Lord Jesus. When we are home, we will still say, "Lord Jesus, I love You."

Brother John Nelson Darby lived to be over eighty-four years of age. One day when he was quite old, he was traveling and stayed overnight in a hotel. Before going to sleep, he said to the Lord, "Lord Jesus, I still love You." None of his writings inspired me as much as this single short sentence. That short word touched my heart. By that time he was quite old, yet he could still speak such a word to the Lord. It was many years ago when I read this. I immediately told the Lord, "Lord, keep me loving You all the time. I just ask You to do this one thing."

FOLLOW AFTER LOVE

Give yourself to love the Lord. No other way is so prevailing, and no other way is so safe, so rich, and so full of enjoyment. Just love Him. Do not care for anything else. Teachings, doctrines, gifts, and power do not mean much. We must continually tell the Lord, "Lord, keep me in Your love! Attract me with Yourself! Keep me all the time in Your loving presence!" If we will pray in this way, we will see what love we will have toward the Lord and what kind of life we will live. We will simply live by the Lord Himself. As long as we love Him from the deepest part of our being, everything will be all right. If we need wisdom, He will be the wisdom to us. If we need power, He will be the power. If we need the proper and adequate knowledge, He will even be that to us. Whatever we need, He is. Do not try to get anything else; just look to Him that He would reveal His love to you. Song of Songs 1:4 says, "Draw me; we will run after you." We must ask the Lord to draw us, and then others will run after Him with us. To take Him as our life, we must love Him in such a way.

In Revelation 2 the degradation of the church began with the loss of the first love toward the Lord Jesus. The church in Ephesus had many good works and was even strong in faith, but the Lord rebuked her by saying, "I have one thing against you, that you have left your first love" (v. 4). They had lost the fresh and best love toward the Lord. This started the degradation of the churches. When we lose our love for the Lord, we start to backslide. We must go to the Lord and make a deal with Him: "Lord, be merciful to me! I do not need anything or anyone else but Your loving self. Simply show me Yourself! Draw me that we may run after You. O Lord, show me Your love that I might be constrained by Your love! I do not want to do anything for You, Lord. I just want to love You. I just want to take You as my person. I want Your personality as my personality, Your will as my will, Your desires as my desires. I want Your everything as my everything."

Thus, we see that it is not simply a matter of believing but also a matter of loving. We must learn to love the Lord Jesus. If we have such a burning love toward the Lord Jesus, we will enjoy all that He is. Therefore, I do not encourage you to seek anything else. Go to the Lord and ask Him to draw you that you may run after Him. You must realize that the zoe life is such a loving, wonderful person and that love is the way to deal with Him.

CHAPTER THREE

LOVING THE LORD FOR HIS PURPOSE

Scripture Reading: S. S. 1:2-4, 13-14; 2:3-4, 8-10, 16-17; 3:1-4

RECEIVE AND ENJOY

We have seen that to believe in the Lord is to receive Him, and that to love Him is to enjoy what we have received. So many Christians have believed in the Lord and received the Lord, but not many enjoy the Lord by loving Him.

In John 14:21 and 23, the Lord said that when we love Him, He will manifest Himself to us. This is a personal matter. Then He said that He and His Father will come to us and make an abode with us. This really means a mutual abode. He will be our abode, and we will be His abode. It is a mutual abiding involving persons. A person comes to make His abode with us; hence, we must take the Lord as a person. This abounding grace is not only in faith but also in love.

When Saul of Tarsus was persecuting the Lord, the Lord came to him as a great light, and he was smitten to the earth. Then Saul called, "O Lord, who are You?" And the Lord answered that He was Jesus, the One whom Saul was persecuting. But just by that calling, "O Lord," Jesus came into His persecutor and turned him into one who loved Him.

This is really grace. It is grace that causes us not only to believe in Jesus but also to love Him. For this reason, Paul says that the grace of the Lord superabounds with faith and love (1 Tim. 1:14).

Then Paul says in Galatians 2:20, "...who loved me and gave Himself up for me." Paul is saying that since Christ loved him, he must love Christ. His love constrained Paul to love Jesus. In this way Paul took the Lord Jesus as his life.

There is much talk today about Christ as life, but not many Christians really know how to enjoy the Lord as life. It is not a matter of knowing but a matter of enjoying. Yes, Christ is our life, but how can we enjoy Him as our life? There is no other way except by loving Him. This life is not a doctrine; this life is a person. If we would enjoy Him as our life, we must take Him as our person. The One who is our life is a living person! Therefore, we must love this person.

PERSONALITY PROBLEMS

To love a person is wonderful, but it also causes problems. I have been loving this particular Bible since 1964. For the past eight years, I have never had any problem with it, because it is not a person. There is no problem to love something that is lifeless. But when you love a person, there are always problems. All of us who are husbands do love our wives, yet loving our wives oftentimes causes problems. And the more we love them, the more problems we have. This Bible has never given me any problem because it has no personality, but the more the wives and husbands love each other, the more trouble they have.

Generally speaking, you never hate a person whom you have never loved. Loving a person really involves something. The more you love, the more problems you will have. You will never hate a stranger walking on the street; it is always those with whom you have close contact, such as your roommate or your marriage mate. First we love them, but then our love issues in problems. I have never met a husband who had no problems with his wife, and I have never met a wife who had no problems with her husband. It is because they love one another as a person. If we did not have love, there would be no problem; but because the one we love is a person, there are problems. Because I am a person, I cause problems for my wife and for those with whom I am closely associated. While we work together and love one another, we experience some problems.

THE STRONGEST PERSON

The stronger a person is, the more problems he will give

you if you love him—and Jesus is the strongest person. A Bible does not cause problems because it has no personality; it is not a person. Some persons are weak; with such weak persons there are hardly any problems. The husbands have problems with their dear wives because their wives are so strong. It is even worse for the wives, because their husbands are stronger than they are. We all must realize, however, that Jesus is the strongest One. Do you think you could subdue Him? You cannot subdue Him; instead, you will be subdued! On the one hand, He is so tender, kind, and humble, but on the other hand, He is never weak. Many wonderful words can be used to describe His personality, but weakness is not one of them. He is always strong, and He is stronger than we are.

Then what shall we do? Though we say that we love Jesus, and we really mean it, we have a real problem: we are loving the strongest person with the strongest personality. Suppose I am very strong, yet someone says that he loves me. His love for me will cause him problems. My strong character and personality will cause him to suffer. After three days, he will forget his love for me. Our love for a Bible will never present any problem, but our love for a person will give us many problems. Moreover, the stronger the person is, the more problems we will have.

THE SONG OF SONGS

This is why we want to see something from the Song of Songs. Many of us, after reading the above verses, will think that this is a wonderful book about loving Jesus. Yes, it is indeed a wonderful book. But many times the record in this book is not so exciting; instead, it is rather disappointing. All the above verses have some exciting points, but the main point in quoting all these verses is not to show us the exciting points but the disappointing ones.

SEEKING AND FINDING THE LORD

"Let him kiss me with the kisses of his mouth! / For your love is better than wine. / Your anointing oils have a pleasant fragrance; / Your name is like ointment poured forth; / Therefore the virgins love you. / Draw me; we will run after you— / The king has brought me into his chambers— / We will be glad and rejoice in you; / We will extol your love more than wine. / Rightly do they love you" (1:2-4).

Here is one who has begun to seek after the Lord. Surely, before the seeking, there was the attracting. Since the Lord has attracted this one to Himself, she is seeking after Him. So she says, "Let him kiss me with the kisses of his mouth!" She must have received a revelation of the Lord's beauty. Our love does not depend so much upon our ability to love the Lord as it depends upon His loveliness. If something is ugly and dirty, we cannot love it. But something so sweet and precious can attract us, even if we have no intention of loving it. Therefore, it is not a matter of our being able to love the Lord but a matter of His being altogether lovely! We cannot love the Lord without seeing His beauty. But once we see His beauty, we cannot help loving Him. He is the most attractive and attracting One. No one can resist the Lord's beauty. When we are attracted to Him, we have to say with this seeking one, "Let him kiss me with the kisses of his mouth!"

After the seeking comes the finding. This one found the one whom she was seeking. The king brought her into his chambers. So in these three verses there are the seeking and the finding.

THE APPRECIATION AND ENJOYMENT

Then in verses 13 and 14 is the appreciation. "My beloved is to me a bundle of myrrh... / My beloved is to me a cluster of henna flowers / In the vineyards of En-gedi." How she appreciates the Lord! He is just like a bundle of myrrh, so sweet inside; and outside He is like a cluster of henna flowers, an Old-World plant with which Jewish girls beautified themselves. She simply appreciates His sweetness and His beauty.

Following the appreciation is the enjoyment: "As the apple tree among the trees of the wood, / So is my beloved among the sons: / In his shade I delighted and sat down, / And his fruit was sweet to my taste. / He brought me into the banqueting house, / And his banner over me was love" (2:3-4). Now her beloved is not only like a bundle of myrrh and a cluster of henna flowers, but he is also like an apple tree with sweet and rich fruit. She is sitting under his shadow enjoying the rest, and she is feeding on his sweet fruit for satisfaction. She is really in the enjoyment.

Do you see the progression in this chapter? It begins with seeking and continues with finding. After finding comes appreciation. Following appreciation is rich enjoyment. It is really wonderful! And the enjoyment is to the fullest, because she not only enjoys him under the apple tree with all the fruits, but she is also brought into the banqueting house, and his banner over her is love. This is enjoyment to the uttermost.

THE SEPARATING WALL

But suddenly there is another picture. "The voice of my beloved! Now he comes, / Leaping upon the mountains, / Skipping upon the hills. / My beloved is like a gazelle or a young hart. / Now he stands behind our wall; / He is looking through the windows, / He is glancing through the lattice" (vv. 8-9). The picture has changed. Now her beloved is leaping upon the mountains and skipping upon the hills. You may think this is wonderful, but if you were the seeking one, you would say, "I am here resting, and he is there jumping and skipping. While I am resting, he is leaping upon the mountains and skipping upon the hills. How different he is from me."

A short while before, he was with her in the banqueting house; now, she is still in the house while he is outside the wall. A wall is separating them; he is behind the wall. This portrays some separation between the seeking one and the Lord. In the banqueting house they were one. But now she is within the wall, and he is outside the wall; she is resting, and he is jumping, leaping, and skipping.

So you see, it is possible that while we are loving Jesus, He is away from us. He may not be far away, but there is a separation, a wall between Him and us. He was with us in the banqueting house, but now there is a wall between us. It was so wonderful to be in the banqueting house, but now while we are still inside, He is outside. We are still resting and enjoying, but He is leaping and skipping. We have our character, and He has His. While we have our resting personality, He has His skipping personality.

But praise the Lord that walls nearly always have some openings. He can still see the seeking one by looking through the window. Praise the Lord for the window; but there is a lattice. He can see through, but He cannot get in. This is really meaningful. The Song of Songs is poetry, and a picture is portrayed here. There is a wall with a window, but the window has a lattice. Many times our experiences with the Lord have been just like this. While we were so much in love with Him, He was not with us. He was outside the wall. We were within, and He was without. But an opening was there for Him to see us and for us to see Him. However, He could not get in, and we could not get out because of the lattice.

Many times in our experiences with the Lord, something like this will happen. We are separated, but we can still see through. Yet we cannot get through, and the Lord cannot get through either. But the seeking one did hear His voice. She said, "The voice of my beloved!" She heard His voice, and He seemed to be saying, "Rise up; don't rest anymore. Come out of the house; don't remain in your situation."

THE REAL TEST

This is the real test. We say that we love the Lord, but we love Him in our way. We love Him according to our taste, our intention, and our goal. We do not love Him according to His way, His taste, His intention, or His goal. Our intention is just to enjoy rest and satisfaction, but suddenly Jesus is away. We are satisfied, but He is away. So many dear ones become excited when they come to the local church and touch the Lord's love. But then, after a time, they ask, "What happened?" It seems that the happiness is gone. At first they were so happy—they were even in the heavens—but now the happiness is gone. This is the test. We love Him, but it seems that He is away. We love Him, but we do not have His presence. This is because we have loved Him for our goal and for our intention. He is the Lord. He is the King. His intention is *the* intention. His goal is *the* goal. If we love Him, we must do so according to His intention and for His goal. This is why He says, "Rise up, my love, / My beauty, and come away." This is to call us away from our situation.

A CONTROVERSY BETWEEN TWO PERSONALITIES

Do you see the discrepancy between the Lord and the seeking one? She intends to have rest and stay at home, but the Lord intends that she rise up and go away. The controversy between the two parties is caused by two different personalities. She is a person, and He is also a person. Yet He is a stronger person, and He asks her to rise up and come away. Then she answers, "My beloved is mine, and I am his; / He pastures his flock among the lilies. / Until the day dawns and the shadows flee away, / Turn, my beloved, and be like a gazelle or a young hart / On the mountains of Bether" (vv. 16-17).

The Lord calls her to come away, but she does not care for His calling. She says, "My beloved is mine. He is for me. I just enjoy Him." He asks her to rise up, but she says that He is for her enjoyment and satisfaction. He is the shepherd among the lilies, and she is one of the little lilies under His shepherding. She does not care at all for the Lord's call. She only cares for her enjoyment. She realizes that she is the Lord's, so she says that He is hers and she is His. She was enjoying the Lord's shepherding, the Lord's satisfaction, and the Lord's rest. The picture portrays that she cares only for her own satisfaction. She does not care for the Lord's will, intention, or goal.

But that is not all that she says to the Lord. She also says, "Until the day dawns and the shadows flee away, / Turn, my beloved, and be like a gazelle or a young hart / On the mountains of Bether." This means that she is not ready or willing to go out with the Lord. So she tells the Lord to wait until the shadows flee away. She realizes that some kind of shadow, some kind of darkness, is between her and the Lord. So she tells the Lord to wait for some time, and then to turn back at the mountains of Bether. The word *Bether* means "separation."

Then, in the following chapter the Lord disappears. "On my bed night after night / I sought him whom my soul loves; / I sought him, but found him not. / I will rise now and go about in the city; / In the streets and in the squares / I will seek him whom my soul loves. / I sought him, but found him not. / The watchmen who go about in the city found me— / Have you seen him whom my soul loves? / Scarcely had I passed them / When I found him whom my soul loves; / I held him and would not let go" (3:1-4).

The seeking one seeks the Lord, but she cannot find Him. Finally, she is forced to rise up and go after the Lord. Even though she says that she is not ready and that the Lord must wait until the shadows flee away, the Lord will not go along with her. So He disappears, forcing her to fulfill His call to rise up and go away from her home. She goes into the street and does her best to find her Beloved, but she cannot find Him. Then suddenly, the Lord is there again.

BEING SUBDUED

Do you see the picture? It is right that we should love the Lord, but we should not do it according to our way and our intention. Our will must be subdued to His will. Simply to love Him is not enough. Loving Him will cause many problems. Therefore, we need the subduing of our will. The person whom we love is the strongest One. He will never be subdued, and He can never be subdued. Therefore, we are the ones who must be subdued.

The Lord did not appear to her according to her way or her intention. It was when she was disappointed that He suddenly appeared. But when she found the Lord, she held Him and would not let Him go. This shows her strong character. She was still so strong to hold the Lord according to her way. This whole picture shows us one who has never been subdued. Yes, we love the Lord, yet we have never been subdued. To love the Lord is wonderful, but it also causes problems. The problems are solved only by our being subdued. We must be subdued and conformed to His personality, His will, His intention, and His goal. Otherwise, we will constantly have a controversy with the Lord.

The main problem with husbands and wives in their marriage life is the controversy between them. The wives love their husbands, but they love them according to their own way. The husbands have their way, and the wives have theirs.

The wives' will would never be subdued to the husbands' will, so there are problems. This is why in a wedding the bride always has her head covered to show that she must be subdued.

There is no other way for us to take Christ as life except by loving Him as a person. And if we would love Him as a person, we must be subdued. This is the unique problem between Him and us. There is hardly another problem. The problem is that we are not willing to be subdued, and the Lord Jesus will never be subdued by us. He is humble, kind, and tender, but He will never be subdued. He is the Lord; He is the King; He is the Head. We need to be subdued. This is why I say that all these exciting verses eventually reveal something that is quite disappointing.

Here is a person who loves the Lord, yet a controversy exists between her and the One she loves. Do you think that holding the Lord in such a strong way is good or bad? On the one hand, it is good, because she is holding the Lord. But on the other hand, it is not so good, because she is too strong! The Lord would say, "Please give Me the liberty. Release Me. Don't hold Me so strongly." But because of her strong personality, she holds the Lord very strongly and tells Him that she will never let Him go.

LESSONS IN THE SONG OF SONGS

We love the Lord, but we have a stubborn will and a strong character, which are a real problem to the Lord. We seek the Lord, but we seek Him for our own will and for our own good. This is why in the Song of Songs the Lord must teach His seeking one some lessons. If we read this book carefully, we will see that at the end of the book she is so soft and submissive. Her character and personality are hardly noticeable. What she has is the Lord's character and the Lord's personality. Now she is really one with the Lord. There are two persons but only one personality.

After we are attracted by the Lord's beauty to love Him, we must learn one unique lesson—to be subdued. To take Christ, the living person, as our life requires us to be subdued.

Simply to love Jesus is not enough. The Lord's intention is that we take Him and experience Him as our life. There is no other way except to love Him and be subdued by Him. Then we will be one with Him, having one personality. We will be so soft and submissive to Him. In this picture, the lover of Jesus is exceedingly strong at the beginning, with such a stubborn character. Yet at the end, she is so soft and submissive. This is the lesson that we all must learn in order to really experience Christ as our life.

CHAPTER FOUR

HOW TO TAKE CHRIST AS LIFE

Scripture Reading: S. S. 1:9-11, 15; 2:2, 14; 3:6-7a, 9, 11

Two books in the Bible are closely related: the Gospel of John, which tells us how to take the Lord Jesus as our life, and the Song of Songs, which deals with loving the Lord. Apparently, these two books have no relationship with one another, but in experience we have found that the real way to enjoy the Lord as our life is found in the Song of Songs. If we would pray over the eight chapters of this book in the spirit, we would see how to take the Lord as our life. It does not speak about taking the Lord as our Savior or our Redeemer but as our life.

In this book a seeking one is hungering and thirsting after the Lord. She loves the Lord, and she is seeking the Lord. Actually, this is just enjoying the Lord as life. This book is not about a work or an enterprise; it speaks of a walk that is always seeking after the Lord. It seems that the seeking one has nothing to do except to seek after the One whom she loves. There is nearly no work involved and nothing to do but to seek after such a wonderful person.

THE UNIQUE BOOK FOR LIFE

The Song of Songs is the unique book in the Bible showing us the proper way not only to love the Lord but also to enjoy Him as our life. We all know these verses: John 14:6, "I am... the life"; John 11:25, "I am the resurrection and the life"; John 10:10, "I have come that they may have life and may have it abundantly"; John 1:4, "In Him was life, and the life was the light of men"; and 1 John 5:12, "He who has the Son has the life; he who does not have the Son of God does not have the life." So many Christians know all these verses, but it is not a matter of knowledge; it is a matter of enjoying Christ as life. Many Christians know that Christ is life, but how many of them enjoy Him as life? The way to enjoy Christ as our life is revealed in this book, the Song of Songs.

What is found in the Song of Songs is also found in the Gospel of John in principle, but it is difficult to find unless you first see something in the Song of Songs. Apparently, the Song of Songs is merely a book on loving and seeking the Lord. But I can testify that no other book among the sixty-six books of the Bible has been so helpful to me in the matter of life as this book. I have spent more time in this short book than in any other book of the Old Testament. If we really desire to experience Christ as our life in a way of enjoyment, we cannot stay away from this book.

ONE LESSON

As I have mentioned previously, in the entire book of eight chapters, the Lord is mainly teaching the seeker a unique lesson. Here we have one who is seeking the Lord and who finds Him. After she finds Him, she has the appreciation and enjoyment. Whoever really seeks the Lord will find Him, because the Lord has promised this in Matthew 7:7. If we seek the Lord, surely we will find Him. He will never disappoint us. And the one who loves Jesus in this book is seeking Him in a wonderful way. "Let him kiss me with the kisses of his mouth! / ...Draw me; we will run after you." Immediately, she finds the one whom she is seeking, and he brings her into his inner chambers. Then she has the appreciation. The seeking one says that her beloved is just like a bundle of myrrh and a cluster of henna flowers.

Chapter 2 then tells us of the enjoyment. He is not only the bundle of myrrh and the cluster of henna flowers but also the apple tree in the woods. How enjoyable it is to sit under His shadow for rest and to eat His fruit for satisfaction! This is real enjoyment. She sought the Lord, she found the Lord, she appreciated the Lord, and she really enjoyed the Lord. Hallelujah! He is satisfied, and we are satisfied! What else do we need? It seems that there is nothing left to say but, "Hallelujah!"

THE TURNING POINT

But suddenly the Lord is gone. She was in the banqueting house with such a rich enjoyment, but He was outside. What happened? This is the point of this book. If we are going to enjoy the Lord as life, we must see this discrepancy. The seeking one was enjoying the Lord in such a rich way in the banqueting house. She had the rest and the enjoyment. She was satisfied. But suddenly, while she was resting, He was leaping and skipping. What a discrepancy!

Song of Songs 2:8 is an important turning point in this book. Suppose you were the one in the banqueting house. Would not that be wonderful! Many of you who are in the church life have been brought to such a position. You have arrived in the banqueting house, and you have already discovered that the Lord is gone. You are still in the banqueting house, but His presence is gone. Perhaps two months ago He was with you, but now He is not. Perhaps last year He was with you in the banqueting house, but this year He is not. You would say, "What's wrong? I am still so much for Him. I am still seeking Him, and I am still enjoying Him. But something is missing. He is still lovable, but there is something separating us. I don't love the world. The world is through with me, and I am through with the world. If someone were to give me the world, I simply wouldn't want it. I just love my Lord."

I do believe that by the Lord's mercy so many dear ones in the church life today would say these things. Yet something is missing. He is out, and you are still in. You can see Him, and He can see you, but it seems that there is still some distance between Him and you. I have been asked by so many concerning this one thing, but I have never answered, because I knew that the answer would be given when we covered the Song of Songs.

THE MAIN HINDRANCE TO THE LORD AS LIFE

What is the problem? Before answering directly, we need to see something in the Gospel of John. John 11 records the case of a dead man. Jesus is life, but how could this dead man experience Jesus as life? John 11 shows us a real discrepancy between the lovers of Jesus and Himself, and this discrepancy is exactly the same as in the Song of Songs. Martha is the best representative. She represents you and me. Martha and her sister, Mary, along with Lazarus, their brother, really loved the Lord Jesus. I do not believe that you and I could love the Lord Jesus more than they did. Lazarus became very sick, and Martha and Mary sent a petition to the Lord Jesus for Him to come and help them. But it seems that the Lord did not have any human feeling. He was just like a piece of wood or stone. He heard their petition, but He did not go. He did nothing, and He said nothing. Many times the Lord will remain silent, and at those times His silence is more important than His utterance.

Then after a few days, the Lord decided to go. But Martha did not thank the Lord for His coming. She did not say, "O Lord, how marvelous that You have come! Thank You for Your presence." Instead, she complained that the Lord did not come soon enough. "Lord, if You had been here earlier, my brother would not have died." This means that she put the whole blame upon the Lord. They thought, "Now what is the use for Him to come? Lazarus is already dead." At the time they wanted Him to come, He did not come. Now when they did not need Him anymore, He came. Then the Lord told her, "I am the resurrection. It is not a matter of time, whether it is too early or too late; it is a matter of Me. I am the resurrection. If I came five days ago or three days ago, it would be the same. Now that I have come a few days later, it is also the same. I am the resurrection, and your brother will rise again."

Then Martha became the best expounder of the Bible, for she really knew the doctrine of resurrection. She said, "Yes, Lord, I know that he will be raised up at the last day. We know that doctrine already." Then the Lord said nothing more to her, but Martha went to tell her sister that the Lord had called her. It was not, however, the Lord who had called her, but Martha.

Finally, the Lord came to the grave, and Martha voiced

her opinion again. "Lord, he's stinking by now. He's been in the grave four days." But do not laugh at Martha. Laugh at yourself. She represents all the believers who love the Lord. We do love the Lord, but like Martha, we are always the greatest hindrance to His being our life. This is because we have never been subdued. Our personality and character have never been dealt with. To take the Lord as our life, we must take His character and His personality as our personality. It is not enough simply to quote Galatians 2:20: "I am crucified with Christ; and it is no longer I who live, but it is Christ who lives in me...who loved me and gave Himself up for me." We must repudiate our personality and take Him as our unique person. Then we will have no concepts or opinions, for our personality will be gone. He, as a living person, will be our life.

If Martha had really learned the lesson, she would not have asked the Lord to come in that way. She would have said, "Lord, we would like for You to come. But whether You would come or not, is up to You. Whether You would cause my brother to survive or not, is also up to You. Whether You would do anything, is up to You." To say this is easy, but to learn this lesson and to be brought to this point takes years.

By reading through John 11, we see that Martha did absolutely nothing to help the Lord. Instead, she did everything to hinder and frustrate the Lord from being life to them. If we can see this, it will be easy for us to understand the experience that is recorded in the second chapter of the Song of Songs. The seeker in the Song of Songs is just like Martha. The Lord is training and disciplining the seeking one to forget about herself, her personality, and her will, and to take the Lord Himself as her person.

The Song of Songs mainly teaches us this one unique lesson. Strictly speaking, it is not a book of love. It is not a matter of learning the lesson of faith, patience, or how to become more powerful. For so many years, the Lord will train us in one thing: to put our personality aside and to take Him according to *His* intention, *His* way, and for *His* goal.

Many people love the Lord, but few of them really know

how to take the Lord as life by forgetting their self and their personal character. And so many do not have any intention to learn this lesson. Just as the seeking one in the Song of Songs, they have no intention of responding to the Lord's call.

THE LORD'S APPRAISAL OF THE SEEKING ONE

Now we need to see a little more in these chapters. In all the above verses, the Lord Jesus appraised the seeking one in a certain way.

A Mare among Pharaoh's Chariots

The first appraisal is in 1:9: "I compare you, my love, / To a mare among Pharaoh's chariots." The mare here signifies our natural strength. She is so powerful, but natural and worldly. Pharaoh, the king of Egypt, had the strength that belongs to the world. Some are so strong and powerful, but in a natural and worldly way, like a mare among Pharaoh's chariots.

Doves' Eyes

Then in verse 15, the Lord speaks of the eyes of a dove. "Oh, you are beautiful, my love! / Oh, you are beautiful! Your eyes are like doves." Now the seeking one is making some improvement. When she first sought the Lord, she was as strong as a mare. But now she has gradually learned to look upon the Lord with doves' eyes.

A Lily

After this, the Lord likens her to a lily. "As a lily among thorns, / So is my love among the daughters" (2:2). The Lord spoke of a lily in Matthew 6 as one who lives on this earth not trusting in his own strength but upon God's mercy. At first she was as strong as a mare, naturally. However, now she no longer trusts in her natural strength, but she trusts in the Lord's mercy. She is just a lily trusting the Lord for everything.

A Dove

From a lily, the seeking one continues to improve to become a dove. "My dove, in the clefts of the rock, / In the covert of the precipice, / Let me see your countenance, / Let me hear your voice; / For your voice is sweet, / And your countenance is lovely" (S. S. 2:14). First of all she only had doves' eyes, but now she is a dove. Which is more powerful, a mare or a dove? And which would you rather be? I believe that most of us would like to be a mare that is so powerful and full of strength. A dove is small and not so powerful. But to go on from a mare to a dove is a real improvement. I hope that in the local churches there will be many doves and not so many mares. I am afraid that there are too many mares in the churches. All the mares must be transformed into doves. In the Bible the dove is the sign of the Holy Spirit. When the Lord was baptized, the Spirit descended upon Him like a dove. If we are really in the spirit and one with the Spirit, we will be like a dove. There will be the real improvement.

A Pillar of Smoke, a Bed, and a Palanquin

Between the dove and the next stage, there is a long period of time. I do not know how long a time it takes, but I do know that this period of time between Song of Songs 2:14 and 3:6 is not short. Here we see something wonderful: "Who is she who comes up from the wilderness / Like pillars of smoke, / Perfumed with myrrh and frankincense, / With all the fragrant powders of the merchant? / There is Solomon's bed; / ...King Solomon made himself a palanquin / Of the wood of Lebanon" (3:6-7a, 9).

What a change in the seeking one! Now she comes up from the wilderness, not as a mare, neither as a dove, but as a pillar of smoke. It is smoke, yet it is a pillar, something so solid. Who is this one perfumed with myrrh and frankincense and with all the fragrant powders of the merchant? The question was asked about her, but the answer is made concerning King Solomon. Who is this one? This is Solomon's bed, a place of rest during the night. The seeking one has improved so much that now she has become the Lord's rest. Who is this one? She is Solomon's resting place, and she is Solomon's palanquin. This is a carriage that is carried by men for traveling during the day. The bed is for resting at night, and the palanquin is for moving during the day. Who is this one? She is the resting place of Jesus and the moving carriage of Jesus!

This is really quite deep. It is far more than just the banqueting house. It is not the shade of the apple tree, but the bed of Solomon and the carriage of Solomon. Who is this one? She is just the resting place of Jesus, and she is the carriage of Jesus for His move on this earth. She has become the very expression of Jesus, and by this expression Jesus moves on the earth. During the night, she is His resting place, and during the day, she is His very expression for His move on the earth. Now she has really learned to take the Lord as her life. His personality is now her personality, and His expression is her expression.

A Crown

"Go forth, O daughters of Zion, / And look at King Solomon with the crown / With which his mother crowned him / On the day of his espousals, / Yes, on the day of the gladness of his heart" (v. 11). Ultimately, she becomes the very crown of the Bridegroom. Later, we will consider the crown in greater detail.

> God's life and building can be seen
>   Within the Song of Songs;
> He shows by types His seeking ones,
>   The Bride for whom Christ longs!
>
> She, as a team of horses shows
>   A love, so swift and strong!
> But this is love that's natural—
>   It pulls the world along!
>
> As time goes by, her concepts change,
>   With dove's eyes she can see
> That naught can with her love compare—
>   There's none so dear as He!
>
> A lily she is now to Him
>   (For still the Lord draws on),
> Her faith is not in earthly toil,
>   But in the wondrous Son.

She's next a dove who hides herself
  Within the cloven rock;
Now in her Lord's ascended life
  Is love which knows no shock!

Of smoke, a pillar she's become,
  And now, as wand'ring ends,
Her wills to His will are subdued,
  What fragrance sweet ascends!

Behold His couch...(O, can this be?)
  E'en midst the fearsome night...
She now affords her Lord such rest,
  The foe is put to flight!

A vessel to contain the King!
  (This type is full of worth.)
A palanquin He's made Himself
  For His move on the earth!

                    (*Hymns,* #1241)

Chapter Five

EIGHT STAGES OF GROWTH IN LIFE

Scripture Reading: S. S. 1:9, 15; 2:2, 14; 3:6-7, 9-11

A FAMILY OF DESCRIPTION

In the last chapter we saw the Lord's appraisal of the seeking one in the first three chapters of the Song of Songs.

It is not so easy to understand the Bible. In the last chapter we had a group of words which belong to the same family; I would call it a family of description. The Lord used at least eight figures to describe His seeking one. The Lord's description of His seeker with different figures illustrated the state the seeker had attained at that time. Therefore, if we consider all eight figures together and compare them with one another, we will see their meaning. They indicate the growth in life and the transformation of life.

First of all, the Lord Jesus used the figure of a mare. Next He spoke of the doves' eyes. She was not a dove yet, but she had the eyes of a dove. After the doves' eyes there was the lily. The dove as a complete entity followed the lily. Following the dove were the pillars of smoke, the bed, and the palanquin. Finally, there was the crown. If we pray over these eight figures, I believe that the Holy Spirit will show us something so meaningful. My burden is not to expound the Song of Songs but that we all may know the way to take the Lord's life. So many Christians talk about Christ as life, but very few know how to experience Him as life.

CHRIST AS LIFE

The way to enjoy and experience Christ as life is found in the Song of Songs. The term *life* is not used in this book, but

there is the way to enjoy Christ as life. The way to enjoy
Christ as life is simply to love Him as a wonderful person.
The Gospel of John is not a book of doctrines, gifts, or power;
it is a presentation of a wonderful person. The Song of Songs
is exactly the same. There are not any doctrines in this book
or any doctrinal terms. There are no manifestations of gifts or
power. These eight chapters reveal to us a lovable person. He
is altogether lovely! And this person is not only our life but
also our living. In the Song of Songs, this lovely One is just
the life and the living of His seeker. The seeking one takes
this lovely One as her life within and her living without by
loving Him. Oh, we must love such a wonderful person! Then
we will take Him as our life and as our living. He will become
our talk, our walk, our attitude, our expression, our everything! He will become not only our life within but also our
living without. "To me, to live is Christ" (Phil. 1:21). This is
the Song of Songs.

A CONTINUAL CHANGE

This book not only presents a picture of this wonderful,
loving person, but it also gives a clear picture of the seeking
one who loves Him so much. This is why there is a continual
change in her growth in life. We cannot help growing in life
and having the transformation of life if we really love the
Lord Jesus. If you say that you love the Lord Jesus, yet year
after year you remain the same, I do not believe you. If a
person really loves the Lord, there will be a continual growth
and change in life. It is not by teaching, instruction, correction, or adjustment. I do not have confidence in these things.
They can only adjust a little in an outward way, just as the
morticians do who work on a corpse. They make some
changes, but they are all outward; not one bit comes out of
life. There is no growth, no transformation, no improvement,
no change, and no living progress.

Consider the seeking one in the Song of Songs. All the
time she is growing, changing, and being transformed. What
a transformation—from a mare to a dove! From a dove to pillars of smoke! From the pillars of smoke to the bed! From the
bed to a palanquin! And from the palanquin to a crown! In all

these figures we can see the growth in life of such a seeking one. It is not by teaching, and it is not by gifts. We must realize that no transformation of life can come out of any gifts. In John 2 many people saw the miracles done by the Lord and believed in Him. Yet the Lord would not commit Himself to the miracle appraisers. We should not be miracle appraisers but person appraisers—those who love and seek after the Lord Himself. Then there will be the growth in life and the transformation of life.

NATURAL, WORLDLY STRENGTH

We need to look at all eight figures in more detail. A horse in the Bible always signifies strength and speed (Psa. 33:17; 147:10). This mare is used for the Egyptian king. "I compare you, my love, / To a mare among Pharaoh's chariots" (S. S. 1:9). The mare signifies natural strength in a worldly way. The Lord's seeker is using her strength to seek the Lord. In verse 7 she prayed, "Tell me, you whom my soul loves, Where do you pasture your flock? / Where do you make it lie down at noon?" She prayed for the Lord's feeding and for the Lord's rest. And the Lord answered her in verse 8: "If you yourself do not know, / You fairest among women, / Go forth on the footsteps of the flock, / And pasture your young goats / By the shepherds' tents." She followed in such a strong way that the Lord praised her, saying that she was like a mare among Pharaoh's chariots. This is good but good in a natural, worldly way. You are seeking the Lord, but you drag the world behind you. In your seeking of the Lord, others are impressed not with the Lord but with something of Pharaoh. You are not carrying Solomon but Pharaoh.

Many of the young people in the churches are really seeking the Lord. Yet they pull "the chariots of Pharaoh" with them. Something from Egypt, something from the world, is being pulled behind them. It is not something evil but something of Pharaoh. Sometimes it is quite stately and royal, yet it comes from the world. The young people are attracted by the Lord, and they are loving Him, but they are still the "mare among Pharaoh's chariots," pulling something of the world. They are not like Solomon's palanquin, carrying Christ.

Are we really seeking the Lord? Then whom are we carrying? Are we carrying Pharaoh, or are we carrying Solomon? If
we are bearing Pharaoh, we are a mare used to pull his char-
iot. But if we are bearing Solomon, we are a palanquin, a
vessel for Him. Solomon is contained in this vessel. For the
mare to carry Pharaoh, there is no need of a vessel. But if we
would carry Solomon, we must be a vessel, a container, as His
palanquin.

GROWTH BY APPRECIATION

After the Lord's first appraisal of the seeking one, she
enjoyed the Lord more and more, and she appreciated the
Lord. Between 1:9 and 1:15, there are several verses showing
how the Lord appreciated her and how she appreciated the
Lord. She said, "My beloved is to me a bundle of myrrh / That
lies at night between my breasts. / My beloved is to me as a
cluster of henna flowers / In the vineyards of En-gedi" (vv.
13-14). By these appreciations of the Lord there was the
growth in life and the transformation of life. Real appreciation of the Lord always brings the growth in life and the
transformation of life.

SPIRITUAL INSIGHT

The next figure used by the Lord to describe her is the
doves' eyes. "Oh, you are beautiful, my love! / Oh, you are
beautiful! Your eyes are like doves" (v. 15). She was worldly
and natural, but now she begins to have spiritual insight and
spiritual concepts. The dove signifies the Spirit (Matt. 3:16).
The doves' eyes signify the insight, the understanding, and
the realization of the Spirit.

If I were to speak with some of the young people about
their hair, they would be offended, no matter how much they
love the Lord. This is because they still hold a natural concept about their hair. But if they were to appreciate the Lord
more and more, this appreciation would give them a spiritual
concept and the insight of the Spirit. Their mare's eyes would
be transformed into doves' eyes. Then they would look at
their hair, their sideburns, their mustaches, their eyeglasses,
and their tee shirts in a different way. I know that today's

young people are fond of all these things. They have their natural concepts, but this is like having the wild mare's eyes. But the Lord Jesus is so real. He can convert our sight. He can change our mare's eyes into doves' eyes. The more we appreciate Him, the more our eyesight will be transformed.

The doves' eyes are the spiritual insights that come from continually gazing on the Lord and putting our trust in Him. We no longer trust in our natural mare strength, but now we trust in Him. When the seeking one's eyes have become the eyes of the dove, she has lost her confidence in her natural strength. She has turned away from her natural strength to the Lord and is continually looking unto Him. By her appreciation of Him, she receives the heavenly concept and spiritual insight. Now she has doves' eyes to see things in a new way. She has not yet become a full dove, but she has the eyes of a dove. At least her concept, her insight, and her looking unto the Lord are like the eyes of the dove.

A LIFE OF FAITH

After having the eyes of the dove, she becomes a lily. "As a lily among thorns, / So is my love among the daughters" (2:2). In the Bible, a lily signifies a life lived wholly by faith. The Lord said in Matthew 6:28-30, "Consider well the lilies of the field, how they grow. They do not toil, neither do they spin thread. But I tell you that not even Solomon in all his glory was clothed like one of these. And if God so arrays the grass of the field, which is here today and tomorrow is cast into the furnace, will He not much more clothe you, you of little faith?" A lily is one of the Lord's seeking ones who lives on this earth but not by this earth. She lives by trusting in God; she does not put her trust in this earth. By such a faith she becomes as pure as the white lilies. Such are the pure ones who live by faith in God. Not only does the Lord Himself consider the seeking one in Song of Songs as a lily, but even she herself recognizes that she is a lily. In 2:16 she says, "My beloved is mine, and I am his; / He pastures his flock among the lilies." She is one of the lilies, and among these lilies the Lord is shepherding His flock.

A COMPLETE DOVE

The turn from the doves' eyes to the lily indicates a further improvement. Now she not only looks unto the Lord but also has a practical faith in Him. She not only has lost her natural strength and confidence, but she also has real faith in God. She has put away her trust in her mare's strength, and now she has a living trust in God. She not only has the eyes of a dove but also the pure faith of a lily. Hallelujah! What a picture! After becoming a lily, she becomes a complete dove. "My dove, in the clefts of the rock, / In the covert of the precipice, / Let me see your countenance, / Let me hear your voice; / For your voice is sweet, / And your countenance is lovely" (v. 14).

All the improvements and all the stages of the growth in life can only come as we are taking Christ as our person. We must love Him, appreciate Him, and learn more and more to live by Him. Then we will progress from the mare to the doves' eyes, then to the lily, and eventually to the complete dove. In these stages the seeking one is continually dealing with the Lord. She is learning to take the Lord as her everything, and by this she is growing and improving. There is a continuous transformation from the mare stage to the dove stage.

A LONG PERIOD

But this is not the end. A dove is lovely and gentle but not of much use. After the dove stage there is a long period of time between 2:14 and 3:6. The portion between these two verses shows that a lapse of time has occurred. There are the clefts of the rock, the covert of the precipice, and the myrrh and the frankincense, with all kinds of the fragrant powders of the merchant—all poetic figures describing the death, resurrection, and ascension of the Lord.

STAYING AT THE CROSS

The clefts of the rock signify the cross. Christ was the cleft rock smitten for us (Exo. 17:6; 1 Cor. 10:4). Hence, the clefts of the rock signify His crucifixion, and His crucifixion is just our cross. We must remain in the clefts of the rock; we must stay in His crucifixion. The apostle Paul was always experiencing the death of Christ. He said, "I am crucified with Christ" (Gal. 2:20). He also shared that he was "always bearing about in the body the putting to death of Jesus...We who are alive are always being delivered unto death for Jesus' sake...So then death operates in us" (2 Cor. 4:10-12). This is what it means to be the dove in the clefts of the rock. Only a long period of time in this experience can bring us to the next stage.

Here we need a practical illustration. Suppose I am staying with two brothers. To live together is wonderful, but sometimes it is also horrible. They have their personality and natural makeup, and I have mine. We are all different. Suppose my personality offends this brother's personality. What shall he do? He must say, "O Lord Jesus, keep me in the clefts of the rock; keep me at the cross." By this the Lord will be able to work something into him. In all our different situations, we must stay in the clefts of the rock. "O Lord Jesus, I am crucified with You." To be crucified with Christ on the cross is to stay in the clefts of the rock.

HIDING IN THE LORD'S ASCENSION

We must also stay in the covert of the precipice, where we experience the Lord's ascension. This is mentioned in Psalm 91:1: "He who dwells in the secret place of the Most High / Will abide in the shadow of the Almighty." We all must learn to hide ourselves in the secret place of the Most High. This means to be in the presence of God in the heavenly places, which is to stay in the Lord's ascension. If I am troubled by a certain person or a particular situation, I must pray, "O Lord Jesus, keep me in the clefts of the rock, and help me to stay in the covert of the precipice. O Lord, may I stay at Your cross, and may I stay in Your presence in the heavenlies." In this way I am crossed out, and everything is under my feet. Hallelujah!

This is a wonderful working out of the transformation of life. No one will fail to be transformed by such a life. As long as we are staying at the cross and in the heavenly places in the Lord's presence, there will be a real growth in life and transformation of life.

PERMEATED WITH DEATH AND RESURRECTION

After a long period of such experiences, we come to Song of Songs 3:6: "Who is she who comes up from the wilderness / Like pillars of smoke, / Perfumed with myrrh and frankincense, / With all the fragrant powders of the merchant?" It is better to say "permeated with myrrh and frankincense." We know that in typology myrrh signifies the fragrance of Jesus' death, and frankincense signifies the sweet flavor of His resurrection. We all must be permeated by the flavor of the death and resurrection of Christ. Then we will be perfumed with myrrh and frankincense. This is not just a doctrine to learn; it is an experience that takes time. For many months and years we need to be under the permeating fragrance of the death and resurrection of Christ.

In addition to the myrrh and frankincense, there are also the "fragrant powders of the merchant." Christ is the Merchant, and all His fragrant powders must saturate us. We must be permeated with the death and resurrection of Christ and with all the attributes of the heavenly Christ. This will surely bring about a real transformation.

PILLARS SUPPORTING GOD'S INTEREST

The seeking one has now become pillars of smoke standing on the earth supporting the expanse. The apostles Paul and John were such persons. They were, and still are today, the pillars of smoke in the whole universe supporting the skies. When we read their writings, we realize that they are real pillars to the skies. When we become such pillars, the Lord can commit His purpose to us and upon us. Then we are pillars that stand fast without shaking. This figure is taken from the ancient mode of construction in which they did not use walls to support the building, but they used pillars or columns. Everything rested upon these pillars. This is why Paul mentions Peter, James, and John as pillars of the church (Gal. 2:9). In 1 Timothy 3:15 the church of the living God is spoken of as the pillar and base of the truth. Now the seeking one has become such a pillar to uphold God's interests on the earth.

THE REST OF CHRIST

Who is this one? "There is Solomon's bed; / Sixty mighty men surround it, / Of the mighty men of Israel" (S. S. 3:7). The answer came that she is now the bed of Solomon. The question was about her, but the answer is concerning Solomon. This is because she is now one with Solomon; she is one with Christ. Christ is the content, and she is the container. A bed is a kind of container to hold the content, not for moving but for resting in the night. The mighty men of war surround this bed. This surely means that she has now come into the stage of spiritual warfare. Only the mature ones can fight in the war, and here the war is waged even at night. Yet even during the war in the night, Christ can still have His rest in such a seeking one. Who is this? She is the rest of Christ. She is not only the pillar supporting God's interests on the earth, but she is also the bed affording the rest to Christ, even during the war at night.

Now she is not for her own satisfaction but for Christ's satisfaction. In chapter 2 she was under the apple tree for her satisfaction, but now Solomon lies down and has his satisfaction in her. Who is this one? This is Solomon's bed, his resting place during the war at night.

THE MOVING VESSEL OF CHRIST

She is not only the bed for Solomon to rest in at night; she is also the palanquin for him to move in by day. "King Solomon made himself a palanquin / Of the wood of Lebanon. / Its posts he made of silver, / Its bottom, of gold; / Its seat, of purple; / Its midst was inlaid with love / From the daughters of Jerusalem" (vv. 9-10). The seeking one is now a vessel to contain Christ, carrying Him about in His move. A palanquin is a stately, royal car. As a vessel, it contains the person it carries. She is now the moving vessel of Christ. Christ moves by being contained in her. While she is containing Him, He moves in her and with her. Hallelujah! This is the palanquin of Christ.

The palanquin is constructed of wood, silver, and gold. The wood is the cedar of Lebanon, signifying the Lord's humanity. The posts are silver. Silver always signifies the redemption of Christ. The palanquin is supported by the redemption of Christ. The bottom, the base, is made of gold, which signifies the life and nature of God. God's divine nature is the base.

When we pray-read all these verses, we see how much the seeking one has been transformed. The humanity of Jesus, the divinity of God, and the redemption of Christ are all wrought into her. Only these things can make us a palanquin to Christ. We must have these three materials wrought into us. Then, as His palanquin, we will be built with the humanity of Jesus, the redemption of Christ, and the divine nature of God. It is all very meaningful.

Its midst was inlaid with love from the daughters of Jerusalem. Our midst must be nothing but our love toward the Lord. As a palanquin to Christ, we are decorated and inlaid within with our love toward the Lord. This is why this whole book is a love story. Even when we are transformed to such a stage, our midst must be inlaid with love. This is the palanquin that carries the Lord. It is made of the humanity of Jesus, the redemption of Christ, and the divinity of God; and its midst is inlaid with love to Jesus.

THE WEDDING CROWN

Eventually, such a person becomes the crown. "Go forth, O daughters of Zion, / And look at King Solomon with the crown / With which his mother crowned him / On the day of his espousals, / Yes, on the day of the gladness of his heart" (v. 11). There was the question, "Who is she?" First, the answer came that this was Solomon's bed for resting and his palanquin for moving. Then the answer came that this was Solomon with his crown. She is now the crown of Solomon. If we love the Lord, we will become the crown of Solomon. This is not the crown for kingship; it is the crown at the wedding day. That is the crown for Christ's espousal with us. He is the Bridegroom, and we are the bride. Eventually, the bride becomes the crown to the Groom. Hallelujah!

EXPRESSING ONLY CHRIST

We must see one more thing. When the seeking one was like a mare loving the Lord, she was full of her own opinions. Even as a little dove, she still had a certain kind of personality. However, when she becomes the pillars, the bed, the palanquin, and the crown, she has lost all her personality by being permeated with the myrrh and frankincense, the death and resurrection of Christ. Now she only expresses the personality of Christ in His rest and in His move. This is the way for us to take Christ as our life. It is by loving Him as our person, enjoying Him as our satisfaction, and experiencing Him in so many ways that we may become His full expression.

Chapter Six

THE SUBDUED AND RESURRECTED WILL

Scripture Reading: S. S. 3:6-11; 4:1, 4

A LOSS OF PERSONALITY

In all the figures mentioned in the previous chapter, there is a great change in the character, in the personality, and especially in the will of the seeking one. The first figure is a mare—the strongest of all the figures in personality. If we compare a mare with a dove, the dove has a little character, and it is not strong. And the lily has almost no personality. Hence, of the first four figures—the mare, the doves' eyes, the lily, and the dove—the mare is clearly the strongest in personality. While the lily has almost no personality, something is still there. But in the last four figures—the pillars of smoke, the bed, the palanquin, and the crown—there is definitely no personality. The seeking one's personality has been lost.

Do you think that the pillars of smoke have any personality? And do you think that the bed, the palanquin, or the crown have a personality? It is so clear that the pillars are strong, yet they are without personality. The bed is quite useful in affording rest, but according to the figure, we can see no personality in it. It is the same with the palanquin and the crown. This sequence of pictures from the mare to the crown is quite meaningful and descriptive. At the beginning, the Lord's seeking one was exceedingly strong in her personality, especially in her will. But eventually, by appreciating the Lord Jesus and enjoying His riches, her strong will has been subdued step by step. She stayed in the clefts of the rock and in the covert of the precipice, where she was permeated with the sweet flavor of the death of Christ and the fragrance of His resurrection. This means that the cross and the resurrection life have worked within her to change her character and transform her personality.

To understand such a poetic book with its many figures, we need not only a knowledge of the Bible but also the proper and adequate experience to match our understanding. When all the figures are put together, the picture becomes very meaningful. At first the seeking one is a mare pulling Pharaoh, but eventually she becomes a palanquin containing and carrying Solomon. This picture is better than a thousand words.

TAKING THE LORD AS OUR PERSON

Do you love the Lord? If so, then what stage are you in? Are you as strong as a mare among Pharoah's chariots? Or do you have the doves' eyes? Transformation is always by the renewing of the mind. The transformation of the seeking one began with the changing of her concept. She was like a mare, but she began to have doves' eyes. When your spiritual insight is changed, all outward things seem different. In fact, they do not change; they are just the same. The change is in your concept. Perhaps the movies were very attractive to you in the past. They have not changed, but now they seem so unattractive to you. This is because your eyes have changed. Many of the young people used to love long hair and short skirts. These things have not changed, but their eyes have changed. At the beginning you had mare's eyes, but now you have doves' eyes. You may not have become a dove yet, but your eyes have been transformed. Transformation always begins with our eyes; this is the renewing of our mind. We should not be fashioned according to this age, but we should be transformed by the renewing of our mind (Rom. 12:2). This is to have the mare's eyes changed into doves' eyes.

Then she becomes a lily. Because her concept, ideas, and insight have been changed, she does not trust in the mare's strength any longer. Now she puts her trust in God. She has lost her confidence in the mare's strength. Her strength is still there, but her insight has been turned to another direction. Hence, she is no longer like a mare but like a lily. A mare relies upon its own strength, but a lily must trust in God. This signifies that she puts her trust in God.

This book reveals that to love the Lord Jesus requires us to take Him as our person. But for the Lord to become our person, we need to lose many things. We must lose our insight, our concepts, and eventually our will, our character, and our personality. Then as we progress, we will reach the stage of the pillars of smoke. At that stage no personality is left. It is not an accident that the pillars follow the lily, and the bed comes after the pillars. The first four figures have some amount of personality, but the last four figures have no personality at all. This proves that the more we go on with the Lord, the more we will lose our personality, for the Lord Jesus will be our person.

THE WILDERNESS

By the time the seeking one comes up from the wilderness, she has lost her personality. The wilderness, according to my experience, is just our will. To come up from the wilderness is to come out of the will. The wilderness is really the *will*derness. As long as we are remaining in our will, we are wandering in the wilderness. We could never take a straight path to follow the Lord. Our will becomes a deception to us. Thus, when the seeking one comes up from the wilderness, she comes out of her will. She was like a mare, a lily, and a dove; but now such a strong-willed person has become the pillars.

"Who is she who comes up from the wilderness / Like pillars of smoke?" The answer is that this is Solomon's bed. She no longer has a character or a will. We all know that a bed does not have a will. As long as we have a will, we can never be the resting place of Jesus. To try to rest upon anything with a strong will would be dreadful. But it is easy to rest on a bed, because it has no will. If our bed had a will, it would be impossible for us to rest during the night. But now she has become a bed and a palanquin with no will. And eventually she becomes the crown.

ONE WITH CHRIST

It is quite interesting to see that when the question is asked concerning the one coming up from the wilderness, even the answer shows some improvement. First, she is the bed, then she is a palanquin, and finally, she is Solomon with a crown. She is not simply something with Solomon, but she is Solomon with something. Who is this one? It is just Christ with a crown. She is not only the bed of Solomon or the palanquin of Solomon but also Solomon himself with a crown. This proves that now the seeking one is really one with the Lord. She has become Christ with a crown. Only when we are one with Christ, can He boast and glory in us. Praise the Lord, someday when others ask about us, the answer will be about Christ. We will be Christ with His crown.

THE EXTERNAL STRUCTURE
AND THE INTERIOR DECORATION

With the palanquin there are two aspects: the exterior structure and the interior decoration. Solomon built a palanquin of the wood of Lebanon. This is the substantial structure. Wood signifies humanity, and Lebanon signifies resurrection and ascension. The humanity of the resurrected and ascended Christ is the wood of Lebanon. Christ can make wild mares into a palanquin with His resurrected and ascended humanity. Hallelujah! A mare is something natural by birth; there is absolutely nothing of building up related to it. It is altogether natural. But the palanquin is not something of birth; it is something built up. And the substantial material used for this building is the humanity of Jesus in resurrection and ascension. The moving vessel of Christ is not of natural birth but something built with the resurrected and ascended humanity of Christ.

We should not be shallow. We need to see something substantial, solid, real, deep, and yet so practical. How much we must repudiate our old nature and our own humanity! We must learn to take the Lord's resurrected and ascended humanity as our basic structure so that we may be built into the moving vessel that contains and expresses Him. Moreover, there is not only the wood of Lebanon but also the posts of silver and the golden bottom. Silver signifies the Lord's redemption, and gold, God's divine nature. The redemption of Christ is our supporting strength, and the divine nature of God is the very base of our building.

We need to take all these things to the Lord in prayer so that He may bring us into the reality. We must be such a builded structure, not with our natural strength but with the humanity of Christ, the redemption of Jesus, and the divinity of God.

Solomon made the palanquin himself. It is not that we make it. No one can make such a palanquin except Christ Himself. Throughout the years, the Lord has been working on us with the intention to make a palanquin for Himself. He does not use anything of our natural makeup, but He uses His humanity, His redemption, and the divinity of God.

What is our responsibility? Our responsibility is simply to offer our love to Him. The interior decoration of the palanquin was inlaid with love from the daughters of Jerusalem. We must offer our love to the Lord. He does not want anything from us other than our love. "Simon, son of John, do you love Me more than these?" (John 21:15). He is always seeking our love, and only our love affords something for the interior decoration of the palanquin. The Lord Jesus made it, but it is decorated with our love. The basic structure is of wood, silver, and gold, but our love is the only thing with which the interior is decorated. The more we love Him, the more we will lose our character and personality. The more we love Him, the more we will lose our will, but the interior of the palanquin will be fully decorated.

A WILL OF SUBMISSION

Now we come to Song of Songs 4, which is a continuation of chapter 3. When the question was first asked about the seeking one coming up from the wilderness, the answer did not come from the Lord Himself but from someone else. Then in chapter 4 the Lord gives His answer. "Behold, thou art fair, my love; behold, thou art fair; thou hast doves' eyes within thy locks: thy hair is as a flock of goats, that appear from mount Gilead" (v. 1, KJV). The Lord speaks of her beauty as still being in her eyes, but now something is added. Her doves' eyes are within her locks. I believe that we all know what locks are. It is hair that is curled and put together in a row. Her hair is not left in a loose way. Her beauty is not only in her eyes but in her eyes within the locks. If our hair is loose, there is no way to have locks. The hair must be dealt with in a certain way in order to have the locks.

In this verse I really appreciate the punctuation of the King James Version. After locks, there is a colon, which means "as follows." So the following part of the verse explains what her hair is like. It is like a flock of goats that appears from Mount Gilead. We must realize that this is poetry. It is easy to understand if you have ever seen a flock of goats on a mountain. I saw such a sight both in Scotland and in New Zealand. It does not say that the goats are scattered over the mountain, but that they are flocked together. This is the poetic picture of the hair of the seeking one after becoming the crown. Her hair has been dealt with to become locks, which appear like a flock of goats on a mountain.

We have already seen that the eyes signify spiritual insight; this was the first change in the seeking one. What then does the hair signify? Hair in the Bible always indicates something of the will. All her scattered wills have been gathered together into rows to appear as a flock of goats on a mountain. A flock of goats standing on a mountain presents a picture of submission. Some of the goats are standing on a lower part of the mountain, and some are standing on a higher part. If they were standing on a flat plain, there would be no impression of submission, but for them to be standing on a mountain presents a picture of submission.

The goats are not scattered but gathered; they are not on the plain but on the mountainside, giving a picture of submission. This means that by the improvement from a mare to a palanquin, all the wills of the seeking one have been dealt with. They have been subdued and gathered together to be made into rows full of submission.

Chapter 4 is a continuation of chapter 3. It tells us the secret of how the seeking one made such an improvement: her will was subdued and dealt with. By the time she was the moving vessel of Christ, all her wills had been dealt with and gathered together to present a picture of submission.

THE SUBDUING OF THE WILL

Now we understand what the Lord means when He says, "Behold, thou art fair, my love; behold, thou art fair; thou hast doves' eyes within thy locks: thy hair is as a flock of goats, that appear from mount Gilead." Her beauty is now not only in her insight but in the insight within her locks. Her beauty is seen in her changed concepts within her subdued will. There is not only the renewing of her mind but also the subduing of her will. This is exceedingly fair and comely to the Lord. Formerly, she had only the beauty of the renewing of her mind, but now she also has the beauty of the subduing of her will.

Many times in the past forty years I have come back to the Song of Songs. I have had many experiences in this book, and I have come to realize that it speaks not only of love but also of the subduing of the will. To have complete, adequate, and thorough transformation, there must be the subduing of the will. The more our will is subdued, the more we will be transformed.

Many of us love the Lord, but we still hold on to our will. Our concept has been changed, and our mind has been renewed, but our will needs subduing. Many of us are so stubborn—not only the brothers but also the sisters. The problem is not with our heart. We do love the Lord. I believe that in the past few months the Lord has heard many voices saying, "Lord Jesus, I love You!" But in answer to these voices, I believe the Lord would say, "Yes, I know that you love Me, but what about your will?" To have our concept changed is not enough. We must go on to have our will subdued.

As we have already mentioned, the discrepancy between the seeking one and the Lord in chapter 2 was due entirely to her strong will. The Lord asked her to rise up and come away with Him, but she said that she was not ready. In other words, she was telling the Lord that it was not a matter of His will but her will. Her will was so strong that she would allow the Lord to go away only if He came back when she needed Him. She was even giving orders to the Lord by her strong will. Therefore, the Lord spent a long time dealing with her in the wilderness of the stubborn will. When our will is not subdued, it simply becomes a wilderness to us. The real entering into the good land is a full subduing of our will.

THE WILL IN RESURRECTION

Chapter 3 tells us of the maturity of the seeking one, and chapter 4 continues by explaining how she reached such a mature stage. But this is not all. Eventually, she is reckoned by the Lord as Jerusalem. This is the maturity that is mentioned in chapter 3 when she becomes the palanquin. A palanquin is a miniature of the city. The city contains the Lord in a full way, and the palanquin contains the Lord on a smaller scale. This is the maturity mentioned in chapter 3. Then chapter 4 explains that such a maturity is reached by the subduing of the will.

We also need to read 4:4: "Your neck is like the tower of David, / Built for an armory: / A thousand bucklers hang on it, / All the shields of the mighty men." Here the Lord likens her neck to the tower of David. We have seen that the hair signifies our will, and we know that our neck also signifies our will. Those who are rebellious toward God in the Bible are called stiff-necked (Exo. 32:9; Acts 7:51). So we see that a flock of goats appearing on the mountain shows the subduing of her will, and the tower of David illustrates how strong her will is in resurrection. First of all, our will must be subdued; then it must be strong in resurrection. The natural will must be dealt with, and then we will have a resurrected will. The crucified and subdued will is just like a flock of goats standing on a mountainside, but the resurrected will must be like the tower of David builded up as an armory. An armory is a place where weapons for fighting are kept.

SPIRITUAL WARFARE

How poetic the Song of Songs is! First, our will must be subdued; then it will be resurrected like the tower of David, the armory for the spiritual warfare. All the weapons for spiritual warfare are kept in our subdued and resurrected will. If our will has never been subdued by the Lord, it can never be a strong armory to keep all the weapons for spiritual warfare. All the weapons are mostly defensive, not offensive. It is not so much a matter of going out to fight as it is a matter of standing to resist. Bucklers and shields are all for protection in order to stand. In spiritual warfare, we are not so much on the offensive as we are on the defensive, standing against all the devilish, subtle attacks of the enemy. Most of the items of the armor mentioned in Ephesians 6 are also defensive. There is really no need for us to fight; the Lord has won the battle already.

We simply need to stand and resist all the enemy's attacks. The bucklers and the shields that protect us against the arrows of the enemy are kept in this tower, which is the subdued and resurrected will of the Lord's seeking one. This is the real maturity in life.

An unsubdued will is, on the one hand, stubborn, and on the other hand, weak. When the enemy comes, the stubborn, unsubdued will always makes an unconditional surrender. We all know this by our own experience. This is especially true with the sisters. The sisters who are stubborn in the matter of submission are the first to surrender when the enemy attacks. But if we have a submissive will, a will that has been subdued like a flock of goats on a mountain side, our will is expressed like a tower of David. When the enemy comes, our will is like the tower of David that holds all kinds of weapons against his attacks.

The secret of the maturity of the seeking one in chapter 3 is that her will has been completely subdued and resurrected. Of all eight figures, the first one is strongest in the will, and the last one has no will of its own at all. The mare has an exceedingly strong will, but the palanquin and the crown have no will at all. She has come out of her natural will and is now standing in her resurrected will against the enemy. She is like the tower of David builded as an armory for the spiritual warfare.

CHAPTER SEVEN

THE MOVE OF A LIVING PERSON

Scripture Reading: S. S. 1:4a, 7a, 8a, 9, 12-16a; 2:2-4, 14, 16; 3:6; 4:1; Jer. 50:19; Micah 7:14

THE NEED OF A LIVING PERSON

We have already seen many points about how to take Christ as our living person in the Song of Songs. Many people have misused the Bible as a book of doctrine to form a Christian religion. A religion has doctrines, activities, programs, and works. For the works and activities, there is the need of power to accomplish them and the need of gifts as the ability to perform them. Christianity has mainly these four things: doctrines, activities, the power for the activities, and the gifts.

But strictly speaking, the Lord Jesus is not any kind of religion. The Lord Jesus is a living person! Doctrines are needed with any religion but not with a person. A wife does not need a book of doctrines about her husband because he is a living person. If we are really in the presence of the Lord Jesus, we do not need doctrines. He is our living doctrine. So many hold the doctrine of sanctification, but they are not sanctified, because sanctification is simply the Lord Jesus Himself. You may hold the doctrine of sanctification and yet not have the reality of sanctification. But as long as you have Christ, though you may know nothing of the doctrine of sanctification, you have it! This is because the real sanctification is Christ as a living person.

People today pay too much attention to doctrines, activities, power, or gifts. But what we need is a living person! People can misuse some of the other books in the Bible, but they can hardly misuse the Song of Songs because this book is not of doctrine, activity, power, and gifts. It depicts a living person! "Let him kiss me with the kisses of his mouth! / For your love is better than wine." Anyone who speaks like this is absolutely out of religion.

THE RECOVERY OF A LIVING PERSON

Many people today are for religion, not for a living person. But in the Lord's recovery today, the Lord is not going to recover any religious matter. The Lord is recovering His living person! It is not a recovery of doctrines, forms, or gifts.

When the Lord first came to earth, He was apparently only a little man from Nazareth. But actually, He was also God. John 11 and 12 tell of His being in the house of Mary, Martha, and Lazarus in Bethany. *Bethany* means "house of the poor." He was in the house of the poor, while all the Jewish leaders and priests were offering sacrifices and burning incense to God. They did not realize that the very God whom they were worshipping was in that little cottage. He was not in the temple receiving their worship; He was in the house of the poor ones at Bethany. The very God was there in the form of a little man. Those Jewish worshippers were diligently worshipping God, yet they never realized that God was not there. That was because they were for their religion and their fathers' traditions.

The Lord Jesus came as God to recover His living person to a group of young people. He never went to the temple and called any of the priests to come and follow Him. Instead, He went to the seashore of Galilee and called some rough, young fishermen. He did not even call their fathers. Moreover, all those young fishermen left their fathers; they left all the old traditions, and they followed Him. Today the Lord Jesus is doing the same with the Christian religion as He did with the old Jewish religion.

The Song of Songs is not full of religion with doctrines, activities, powers, or gifts. All that we can find in this book is a loving relationship with a living person! He is both God and man. He is our Creator, and He is our Redeemer. He is our Justifier, our Sanctifier, and our life. He is our Lord, our person, and our everything. We should care for nothing except this living person. As long as we have Him, we have everything. We may not know anything about justification, sanctification, and so many other doctrines. But as long as we have this living person, we have all the doctrines we need.

Suppose we have two men before us. One has a doctor's degree; he has learned many doctrines such as justification and sanctification. But when you talk with him about Christ as a living person, he simply does not know what you are talking about. Although he has studied all the doctrines, he has not once touched the Lord in a living way. The other man has never gained much knowledge. He does not know any of the doctrines, and to him one doctrine is about the same as another. Yet he loves the Lord Jesus. He prays all the time, "O Lord Jesus, how I love You! You are my living person. How I love to touch You!" Do you not believe that he has much more than the first one? It is not a matter of doctrines, teachings, or knowledge. It is a matter of fact. The Lord does not care for our doctrines, teachings, and gifts. He wants to be a living person to us. May the Lord have mercy upon us that we may seek nothing except to gain more and more of Him.

APPRECIATION AND ENJOYMENT

The Lord today is going to recover His living person. In the Song of Songs, we see one who sought the Lord, and by her seeking, she found Him. Having found Him, she began to have sweet fellowship with Him. All of this is in the first two chapters. In her fellowship, first of all, the seeking one had a real appreciation of the Lord. She appreciated the Lord as a bundle of myrrh within and as a cluster of henna flowers without. She sought the Lord, she found the Lord, and in her fellowship with the Lord, she began to appreciate Him. Following this appreciation, there was the enjoyment—she said that her beloved was like an apple tree. An apple tree is not only for appreciation but also for enjoyment. First of all, she had the appreciation, and then she came into the enjoyment of eating the fruit of the apple tree under its shadow. She enjoyed both the fruit and the shadow. After this, she was brought into the banqueting house, which means the house of wine. For her enjoyment, she had something to eat and something to drink. By enjoying the Lord, she began to partake of the Lord.

A PERMEATING WORK

When we eat anything, it becomes a part of us. Whatever we eat enters into us; it is digested and assimilated into our blood stream. Then it becomes our cells and even our organic tissues. Suppose you eat some chicken for lunch. By your eating of the chicken, it gets into you. It is digested and assimilated to become cells in your blood; these cells then become your organic tissue and even your very element. It just becomes you. As we appreciate and enjoy the Lord, something of the element of the Lord is taken into us and eventually becomes us.

The Lord Jesus said, "I am the bread of life...He who eats Me, he also shall live because of Me" (John 6:35, 57b). To enjoy the Lord is to eat the Lord, which means that we take something of the Lord into our being. Then, there will not only be the appreciation and the enjoyment but also the perfuming. To be perfumed means to be permeated with the Lord. This is why we must appreciate the Lord and begin to enjoy Him. By enjoying Him, something of the Lord will get into us to permeate us. This inworking of Jesus is the working of Himself into our being. Eventually, we will be mingled with Him. The Lord is recovering His living person to us so that He may be wrought into our being. This living person is nothing less than God Himself in incarnation, crucifixion, resurrection, and ascension. All these elements are included in His person.

Such a person is going to be wrought into us. He is not just for our appreciation and enjoyment; He must be wrought into us. Then, when the question is asked, "Who is she?" the answer will be that this is Solomon with the crown. We eventually become one with Christ.

DEALING WITH THE EMOTION, MIND, AND WILL

To perfume or permeate any object without any life or personality is quite easy. A ball of cotton put into a bottle of red ink will soon be permeated with the red ink. This is simple. But suppose someone tries to put you as a living person into red ink. Surely you will fight against it. This is why the Lord has a hard time trying to permeate us with Himself. We have our own personality, our own will, and we do not want to lose them.

Therefore, we see in this book that the Lord first touched the emotions of the seeking one. "Let him kiss me with the kisses of his mouth! / ...Draw me, we will run after you." The Lord touched her emotions, and she began to love Him, even though she was as strong as a mare. Then, as she came into the presence of the Lord and began to appreciate the Lord's sweetness and beauty, she was transformed by the renewing of her mind. Her perceptions and her concepts were changed. The Lord first touched her emotions; then He renewed her mind. But this is not all. She still had a strong will. Her emotions were touched, and her mind had been transformed, but her will was still strong. It took a much longer time for the Lord to deal with her will. But eventually, her will became the locks as a flock of goats feeding on Mount Gilead. This was the complete subduing of her will by the cross. Then, in resurrection, her will became as strong as the tower of David to be the arsenal for God.

It was by dealing with the emotion, the mind, and the will, that the Lord was able to work Himself into His seeking one. If we take this merely as a teaching, it will mean nothing to us. By His mercy we must realize that the Lord is speaking to us today. We must begin to love Him with our emotions. Then we will seek Him, find Him, and have sweet fellowship with Him. In the fellowship we will have the appreciation and the enjoyment of Him. Then something of the Lord will get into us to permeate us. This permeating work will transform us and subdue our will. Then we will be willing to let the Lord do whatever He wants. He will put us into the "red ink," and we will be permeated and perfumed. We will be saturated until we have lost our character, our personality, and our will in Him. Then we will really have Him as our person.

A mare has an exceedingly strong personality, but the palanquin does not have any personality of its own, though it does have a personality. Its personality is just the living person it carries. This is why the Lord Jesus wants to work Himself into us to such an extent.

NO SELF EFFORT

After reading these things, we must not try to work them out ourselves. We should not attempt to change our mind or subdue our will. We simply cannot do it. There is only one way to change our mind: by appreciating the Lord. The more we appreciate Him, the more our concept will be changed. Formerly, the movies and all the worldly things seemed attractive to us. Though they have not changed, we simply are not attracted to them anymore. They have not changed, but we have changed. Our concepts have been changed by our appreciation of Jesus. The sweetness and beauty of Jesus have changed our insight. The more we appreciate Him, the more our mind will be changed.

From appreciating the Lord, we must go on to enjoy the Lord. The more we take Him in, the more He will be the permeating element within us. In Him is the myrrh, the frankincense, the clefts of the rock, and the covert of the precipice. All these elements are in His person, and they will be wrought into us until we are transformed and our stubborn will is subdued. The more we feed upon Him and take Him in, the more He will saturate us until our will is completely subdued. This is why the Lord appraised her hair as a flock of goats "that repose on Mount Gilead." Gilead is a place for feeding the flock. "Shepherd Your people... / The flock of Your inheritance, / ...Let them feed in...Gilead / As in the days of old" (Micah 7:14). "I will bring Israel back to his habitation, / And he will feed on Carmel and Bashan, / And...in Gilead / He will satisfy his soul" (Jer. 50:19). There is no other way that our will can be subdued except by feeding on the Lord.

We must not try to subdue our will by ourselves. We must simply learn to feed upon Christ. We must pray-read His Word in a living way, and we must tell Him, "O Lord Jesus, I love You! I take Your very element into me. I feed upon You as the living Word." If we will do this, spontaneously the Lord will permeate our being and subdue our will. Our emotion will be touched, our mind will be transformed, and our will subdued. Then the Lord will have full freedom to saturate us with Himself. We will no longer be a mare but a palanquin and a crown. When anyone asks concerning us, the answer will be that we are simply Christ with the crown. We have been wrought into Jesus, and He has been wrought into us. We are fully one with Him for His move on the earth.

Chapter Eight

THE GARDEN AND THE CITY

Scripture Reading: S. S. 1:11; 3:6, 9-10; 4:4a, 6, 12-16; 5:1; 6:2, 4

LIFE IS FOR BUILDING

We must keep in mind that the theme of all these chapters on the Song of Songs is life and building. It is not only a matter of life but also of building. In the above verses we see something of building. "We will make you plaits of gold / With studs of silver" (1:11). This verse follows the one in which the Lord calls His seeking one "a mare among Pharoah's chariots." As we have mentioned, a mare is something natural, something of birth. There is absolutely nothing of building related to a mare. Therefore, the Lord promises to work on her with gold and silver. Both of these materials are not natural to her. They must be built into her. Here we have the implication that the Lord is going to build something upon her.

All the books in the Scriptures were inspired by God Himself. We see this clearly in the Song of Songs. Not one human being could compose such poetry with all the spiritual applications found in this book. If we did not have the experience and the light from the Lord, even though we were scholars in the language and poetry of this book, I do not believe we could see the real significance here. The real significance is in the matter of building.

From 1:11 we must go to 3:9-10, the verses concerning the palanquin. We have seen that it is built up with wood, silver, gold, and purple, plus the interior decoration. The palanquin has gold as the base, just as the New Jerusalem does. In the New Jerusalem the main part of the city is gold (Rev. 21:18).

In that city is the throne for Christ the King. This is just like
the palanquin, in which there is a purple seat, signifying the
kingship of the Lord. All these materials are for building. The
palanquin is not natural; it has been built up with all these
materials.

Chapter 4 says that her neck is like the tower of David. A
tower is a high building, and this building is for an armory.
By this time, it is clear that the seeking one already has a
certain amount of building. Life comes first, and building follows. Life is for building, and building is the issue of life.

THE GARDEN

After this, the seeking one continues to improve. This is
seen in 4:12-14: "A garden enclosed is my sister, my bride, / A
spring shut up, a fountain sealed. / Your shoots are an orchard
[paradise] of pomegranates / With choicest fruit; / Henna with
spikenard, / Spikenard and saffron; / Calamus and cinnamon, /
With all the trees of frankincense; / Myrrh and aloes, / With
all the chief spices." Now the seeking one is likened by the
Lord to a garden. She is not only a palanquin but also a
garden. The purpose of this garden is mainly for the growth
of certain things.

This corresponds with 1 Corinthians 3:9, which says that
we are God's cultivated land, God's building. God's cultivated
land is equal to the garden. Growing is for building. What is
grown on the farm is for the building of God's house. The
seeking one has become not only a palanquin in which Christ
can move but also a garden to grow so many spices. Eventually, it says this garden is "a paradise" (See footnote 1 on S. S.
4:13, Recovery Version).

Whatever grows in this garden is for the Lord's satisfaction and enjoyment. The Song of Songs begins with eating,
drinking, and enjoyment on the seeker's side, but now the
enjoyment is for the Lord. In chapters 1 and 2 the seeker is
eating the fruit of the apple tree and drinking the wine in
the banqueting house. But now, the Lord is eating the fruits
of the garden and drinking the wine and milk for His enjoyment. "I have come into my garden, my sister, my bride; / I
have gathered my myrrh with my spice; / I have eaten my

honeycomb with my honey; / I have drunk my wine with my milk" (5:1).

THE CITY

In chapter 6 we see the last figure used by the Lord to describe the seeker. "You are as beautiful, my love, as Tirzah, / As lovely as Jerusalem, / As terrible as an army with banners" (v. 4). So we have the garden and the city. Tirzah was the ancient capital of the king (1 Kings 14:17; 16:17-18), and Jerusalem is the holy city of God (Psa. 48:1-2). Therefore, the last figure is really something of building. Now we have ten figures—the first eight, and now the garden and the city.

Besides these ten figures, there are two more: the spring and the fountain. However, for the present we would like to put these two aside. It is clear, in any case, that the Lord Jesus mainly used these ten figures to describe this seeking one. We have become quite familiar with the first eight; now we must see the last two.

GENESIS TO REVELATION

The garden and the city include the whole Bible from beginning to end. The Bible begins with a garden, and it ends with a city. In the first two chapters of the Bible, there is a garden; in the last two chapters, there is a city. In the Song of Songs, the garden and the city are the very person of the seeking one. She fully corresponds now to the standard of God's eternal will. The Bible reveals that God's eternal will is firstly a garden and ultimately a city. This is why this book is so marvelous. The seeker of the Lord in this book becomes these very things—a garden and a city. For this reason we say that the Song of Songs covers the entire Bible. It takes the whole Bible to describe the seeker because the Bible starts with the garden and concludes with the city. Now she is the garden and the city. But this is not all. The name of the garden is Paradise, and the name of the city is Jerusalem. This proves the divine inspiration of the Bible. No human mind could compose a book that fits so well in today's church life. How did Solomon learn all these things? Who told him about life and building? Yet he wrote it all twenty-five hundred years ago. Praise the Lord that He has opened this book to us!

THE CORPORATE BUILDING

Almost all the teaching and edification given in Christianity is for the individual. Everyone is trying to be individually spiritual, and most of the Bible teachers are doing their best to help others to be spiritual in an individual way. But the whole Bible shows us that our spirituality should not be only individualistic. All our spirituality must be for the building. Some of the brothers in the church are carpenters who have helped to build houses and buildings. They know that each individual piece of material is not for itself; every piece is for the corporate building. I never heard anything in Christianity about the corporate building. But I did hear a great deal about this matter from Brother Watchman Nee. For more than three years, from 1939 to 1942, he spoke all the time on the matter of building. At that time the Lord opened up to us the first two chapters and the last two chapters of the Bible. The building in the Bible became so clear to us. But today a message is rarely heard in Christianity about our need to be built up into a corporate Body. May the Lord grant us doves' eyes so that we will have spiritual perception to see that spirituality is not merely for individuals. Spirituality is for the building up of the corporate city.

THE PROGRESSION TO THE BUILDING

The progression to the building is clearly seen in these ten figures. First, there is the mare, then the doves' eyes, the lily, and the dove. After a period of time there are the pillars of smoke. This figure of the pillars indicates building. Then from the pillars we go to the bed and the palanquin. The palanquin is built up with certain materials. Then, comes the crown. All these first eight figures are one group in the first section of this book. The conclusion for this group of figures is the palanquin for the Lord's move and the crown for the Lord's glory. It is really wonderful and marvelous! It seems that the seeking one has reached the peak and that nothing else is needed. If I were the writer of this book, I would probably have closed the book here. It seems good enough to have the palanquin and the crown. But if this is all we have, it is merely individual spirituality, holiness, and maturity in life. Everything is for individuals.

We must realize that this book is divided into two sections. The first eight figures in the first section describe and illustrate the seeking one up to the crown. In the second section, two more figures are used by the Lord to describe this wonderful person: a garden and a city. This is wonderful! If we only had the figures from the mare to the crown, we would have only some pieces and parts of the Scriptures; we would not have the whole Bible. But when we come to the last section of the book, this wonderful seeker becomes the garden and the city. Now she fits into the entire Bible; we can apply the whole Bible to her from the beginning to the end. We can see her in the garden in Genesis 1 and 2, and we can also see her in the New Jerusalem in Revelation 21 and 22. She is both the garden and the city. It is not just a personal, individualistic matter; it is a corporate matter. A garden is for growing, and a city is something built up.

GROWING FOR BUILDING

For us to be the palanquin and the crown of the Lord is indeed wonderful. But we must go on to be the garden. We must grow all the spices, which are the attributes of Christ, the sweet aspects of the Lord's person. The calamus, the cinnamon, the aloes, the myrrh and frankincense, the pomegranate and the henna flower are all different aspects of the Lord's person and work. In the first part of this book, the Lord Jesus was the henna flower to the seeking one. She said, "My beloved is to me a cluster of henna flowers." But now *she* grows henna flowers for the Lord. He was the henna flower to her, and now she grows the henna flowers to Him. He was her enjoyment, but now what He is has been wrought into her, and she is growing it back to Him for His enjoyment. This is really wonderful! And whatever grows out of this garden is the material for the building up of the city. The growing is for the building. We are God's cultivated land to grow the materials for the building up of God's house. This is why we are both the garden and the city. We must grow all the materials for the building up of the city. So the entire book is on life and building. At the end, the seeker becomes a city. This is the last figure used by the Lord to describe His bride. The city, New Jerusalem, is called the bride of the Lamb (Rev. 21:9).

THE MOUNTAIN OF MYRRH
AND THE HILL OF FRANKINCENSE

Now we need to go back to see a few points about the improvement, the progress, and the growth of the seeking one. In chapter 2 she said, "Until the day dawns and the shadows flee away." We know that this really happened. She did have a dawn, and it seemed that all her shadows fled away. She attained to such a place that she became the palanquin and crown to the Lord. But still, in the following chapters, she said the same thing again. "Until the day dawns and the shadows flee away, / I, for my part, will go to the mountain of myrrh / And to the hill of frankincense" (4:6). Regardless of how much we appreciate her as the palanquin and the crown, she herself still realized the existence of some darkness, for shadows were still there. In a sense the day had dawned, but in another sense it had not dawned yet. This is proof that the palanquin and crown are not the consummation of the Christian life. The Christian life must go on to obtain the building. The building is the ultimate issue of all spiritual experiences. However high our experiences are, as long as we have not reached the building, we are still falling short. This is why she still is conscious of some shadows in her life.

What then shall she do? She says that she will go to the mountain of myrrh and to the hill of frankincense. The myrrh and the frankincense had transformed her from her natural state into the palanquin and crown of Christ, and she realizes that they will also take her on. This time, however, she needs to enjoy not just a little myrrh but a mountain of myrrh. It is not a small amount of frankincense but a hill. This is her realization of how much she has experienced the death and resurrection of Christ. But she realizes she still needs more;

she needs even to abide in the death of Christ and in the resurrection of Christ. The death of Christ must be a mountain to her, and the resurrection of Christ must be a hill to her. It is not a small amount but a mountain and a hill. She realizes that she must go there to stay. This was the way she was wrought into the building. In 3:6 she was perfumed with the myrrh and frankincense, but in 4:6 she is going to the mountain of myrrh and the hill of frankincense. When we compare 3:6 with 4:6, we can see the difference. She has come up from the wilderness by being perfumed with myrrh and frankincense, but she still feels that some shadows have not yet fled away. So she goes to the mountain of myrrh and remains there. She goes to the hill of frankincense and dwells there until the day dawns and all the shadows flee away. By staying at the mountain of myrrh and the hill of frankincense, something of God's building is thoroughly wrought into her, and she is fully wrought into God's building. In this way she becomes the garden and then the city.

It is at this stage that the Lord likens her to a garden, and she herself realizes that she is a garden. She invites the Lord Jesus to come to her as to a garden, and He does. "Let my beloved come into his garden / And eat his choicest fruit" (4:16). "I have come into my garden, my sister, my bride" (5:1). The Lord Jesus comes to her as His garden and enjoys the choicest fruit. Now she is not only a palanquin for the Lord's move and a crown for the Lord's boasting but also a garden to grow something for the Lord's satisfaction. All the spices that are grown in the garden are for the Lord's satisfaction and are the materials for building the city.

FULL SATISFACTION

In this book there are many seekings, many findings, and many satisfactions. At least four or five times the seeking one begins again to seek for the Lord. She finds what she is seeking, and she is satisfied. Each satisfaction enlarges her and creates further seeking. She becomes the palanquin and the crown, and in a sense is fully satisfied. Suppose you were to reach such a stage as to become the palanquin and crown to the Lord Jesus. I am sure that you would shout, "Hallelujah!

This is the fullest satisfaction!" But there is still something further and better. We must go on from the crown to grow something for Him as a garden. Then the Lord will find something in us for His enjoyment and His satisfaction. It is not only a matter of being a boast to Him as a crown; we must grow something for the Lord Jesus to eat and enjoy. In other words, we must produce some materials for the building. We are God's cultivated land, and we are God's building. We are the garden, and we are the city. The building of the city comes out of the garden.

THE ARMY

When the seeking one becomes the city, she is also an army. We mentioned that the tenth figure is the last one, but there is also the eleventh. This is the army. "You are as beautiful, my love, as Tirzah, / As lovely as Jerusalem, / As terrible as an army with banners." Why do I say that the tenth is the last, yet there is still the eleventh? It is because the tenth is the eleventh, and the eleventh is the tenth. When we become a city to the Lord, we are an army to the enemy. It is not just an armory as in the past (4:4). An armory is defensive, but the army is offensive. It is not just a matter of defending the kingdom but also of fighting for the kingdom. She is so beautiful to the Lord, even as beautiful as Jerusalem. But to the enemy, she is as terrible as an army with banners. We all know that an army with banners means victory. She is not without banners. This means that she has won the victory already. No wonder she is so terrible to the enemy!

BUILDING AND WARFARE

First, there was the armory for the defensive warfare. But now the seeking one has become an army marching in triumphant victory. The Hebrew word *army* in this verse is in the plural, so some versions say that she is the hosts, the troops. It is not just one troop but the many troops with banners. She has become such a marvelous fighting army as troops with the victory banners. We can never separate the building from the spiritual warfare. Wherever the building is, there is the battle. We all remember the account in Nehemiah: with one hand the people did the building work, and with the other hand they held the weapons for battle (4:17). While they were building, they were fighting. Fighting always accompanies the building, and the building always brings in the victory in the battle. This is the consummation of the Christian life. This is the uttermost completion that the seeking one of the Lord can attain. She is now a city as an army.

In Ezekiel 37:2-10 we read the same thing. All the dry bones, after being inbreathed with life, came alive to be built into the habitation of God. And at the same time they were formed into an army. The building is always an army. Without an enemy, there is no need to build a city. In human history, the city came into existence because of the attacks of the enemies. The city is God's dwelling place, but it is also the fighting army to the enemy.

THE LORD'S RECOVERY

Today's Christianity is very lacking in all these matters. This is why the Lord has still not come back. How can He return without all these things being recovered and accomplished among His people on earth? This is what the Lord is doing in His recovery, and this is why we say that this is not the recovery of doctrine. It is the recovery of life and building. This is His work, which He started in Genesis 1. The enemy has done his best to frustrate it, but the enemy cannot stop the Lord's recovery. Today the Lord is going to recover life and building!

A real warfare is being waged today for the Lord's recovery. Some may think that they have been called for this or for that. But these are just the traditional things. We all have been called for the Lord's recovery. May the Lord have mercy on us that we may see His divine work of recovery and what is missing in today's Christianity.

To love the Lord Jesus does not mean to work for Him. Working for Him means nothing to the Lord Jesus. If you do not believe this today, some day you will believe it. But that day will be too late. It is not that we work for Him but that He works on us. We must not be merely His workers but His

work (Eph. 2:10). We must take in the Lord so that He may
perfume us and transform us. Then we will progress from one
figure to another and will arrive at the stage of the palanquin
and the crown. But we still need to go on to the garden and
the city. May the Lord be merciful to us and take us all the
way! Life and building are the two main items of the Lord's
recovery. This is why we must attain to the garden and the
city.

> To the Lord we're as a garden,
>   Out from which the spices flow;
> All the precious fruits of Jesus
>   Freely in this garden grow.

>   Spikenard, saffron, henna flower,
>   Cinnamon and calamus,
>   Frankincense and myrrh and aloes;
>   O Lord, we would ever grow Thee thus.

> O Lord, come into Thy garden,
>   Come, Beloved, come and eat
> Freely for Thy satisfaction
>   Of Thy fruit, abundant, sweet.

>   "Yea," Thou answerest, "I am eating
>   Honeycomb with honey pure."
>   All sweet spices from Thy garden,
>   Doth Thy satisfaction, Lord, secure.

> All the produce of the garden
>   Is with resurrection filled
> That the Lord may have a city,
>   Fruits of resurrection build.

>   From the garden to the city,
>   Growth transformed to precious stone;
>   Christ is thus expressed, reflected—
>   God in all His glory fully shown.

> Now the city, fair and comely,
>   As the dawn, triumphantly,
> Is an army strong and mighty
>   Marching forth in victory.

Lo, the city and the army—
Saints transformed in one accord.
What a terror to the devil,
And so beautiful unto the Lord!

                    (*Hymns,* #1156)

CHAPTER NINE

THE CORPORATE LIFE
AS SEEN IN THE GARDEN

Scripture Reading: S. S. 4:6-16; 5:1

FROM A MARE TO A CITY

The seeking one in the Song of Songs is likened by the
Lord at the beginning to a mare. The Lord said to her, "I compare you, my love, / To a mare among Pharaoh's chariots"
(1:9). She was a mare, but among Pharaoh's chariots. In the
Bible Pharaoh is related not only to the world but also to
Satan. Pharaoh was a type of the prince of the world. The
Lord appraised the seeking one, yet He was wise. In His
appraisal of her, something was related to the prince of the
world. This indicated that the Lord was saying, "My love, you
do love Me, yet you are still carrying something of the world;
you are still related to the prince of the world. I must liken
you to a mare among Pharaoh's chariots."

But in chapter 6 there is much maturity. It seemed that
she was completely matured in chapter 4, and this was true
to a certain degree. She was indeed matured but not as
matured as she is in chapter 6. In chapter 6 the Lord likens
her to a city with the name of Jerusalem. "You are as beautiful, my love, as Tirzah, / As lovely as Jerusalem, / As terrible
as an army with banners" (v. 4). She is no longer linked with
Pharaoh but with Jerusalem. She is no longer related to the
prince of this world but to Jerusalem. She is not a mare
anymore but a city, and a city with the unique name of Jerusalem. This is the name of a city found both in the Old and
New Testaments. It is a name given by God that will remain
for eternity.

We know of some people today who do not believe that the Bible was inspired by God. But do you believe King Solomon by himself could compose poetry that is so fitting for today's church life? Undoubtedly, the Lord Himself inspired this book. This short book has never been so open and understandable to the Lord's people as it is to us today. Today we are clear that this book describes the love between the Lord and His loved ones.

When we consider all the figures used to describe the seeking one, we marvel: from the mare to the garden, and eventually to the city. And this city is an army. To the Lord she is lovely and beautiful, but to the enemy she is terrible and terrifying. Positively, she is the city to fulfill God's purpose to express Himself, and negatively, she is the army to fulfill His purpose to deal with His enemy. The city expresses God in His loveliness and beauty, and the army deals with God's adversary.

May this not simply be a kind of teaching or saying among us! We must all enter into the experience of these things. We need the revelation, the reality, and the real experiences! How could this seeking one grow so much until she becomes a garden to the Lord? We must see how the garden comes into being. Though we may say that we have seen it, we still need to see something more.

TWO ASPECTS

The first part of this book shows the first aspect of the Christian life; the last part shows the last aspect of the Christian life. Most Christians only care for the first aspect, which is mainly individual. Very few care for the last aspect, the corporate life. We have seen the Christian life in an individual way in the foregoing eight figures. There were the mare, the doves' eyes, the lily, the dove, the pillars of smoke, the bed, the palanquin, and the crown—all mainly a portrait describing the individual Christian life.

If most of us could attain to the transformation of a palanquin or a crown to the Lord, we would consider that to be the consummation of our Christian life. How wonderful it would be if we could be a transformed palanquin for the Lord's move!

To become a crown for the Lord's glory and boast—that would be wonderful! Even the Lord Jesus did not mention any shortcomings in her. The end of chapter 3 shows the appraisal of others. Some asked, "Who is she?" The others answered, "This is Solomon's bed and Solomon's palanquin. It is even Solomon with the crown." Then chapter 4 gives the Lord's appraisal. In both appraisals no shortcomings are mentioned. She has been perfected in her Christian life.

SOMETHING LACKING

Yet, even after all these appraisals, she still says, "Until the day dawns and the shadows flee away, / I, for my part, will go to the mountain of myrrh / And to the hill of frankincense" (v. 6). Regardless of how well others appraise her, including the Lord, she still has the feeling that the day is not dawning and some shadows still exist. So even at this stage she still desires to have a deeper, fuller experience of the Lord's death. Hence, she goes to the mountain of myrrh and the hill of frankincense. This means that she will stay there until her day dawns and all the shadows flee away.

Why, after such an attainment, are there still shadows and no dawn? Because regardless of how high she has attained, the Lord's final purpose has not been fulfilled. As to herself, she has satisfaction and maturity. But concerning the Lord's purpose, nothing has been fulfilled. She has attained to such a high state, yet she still feels that something is lacking. There is still no dawn, and there are still some shadows. So she would take herself to the mountain of the Lord's death and the hill of His resurrection.

THE NEED OF MORE TIME

This kind of experience requires a longer period of time to pass through. No one can tell how long she stayed there. Even today with us, no one knows how long it takes. For some it may be five years, for others seven years, and for others it may be twelve years. We all need a longer time to stay at the mountain of myrrh and the hill of frankincense. One thing is certain: it could never be accomplished overnight. We cannot read another chapter in the Bible and stay in the Lord's presence for another half-hour, and then we have it. No, we have to stay there. It takes time.

Sometimes we are too much in haste. We have to learn to slow down. Many times I was desperate in the Lord's presence, and the Lord told me, "Go to sleep." I was desperate to tell the Lord so many things, but the Lord simply told me, "Go to sleep. Don't worry so much." It takes time. We cannot stretch ourselves on the bed to be a little taller and then expect the next day to have grown half a foot. But if we eat and sleep and exercise, we grow unconsciously, without knowing it. After many years, we will grow into a full-grown man.

TRANSFERRED TO LEBANON

No one knows how long this seeker of the Lord Jesus stayed on the mountain of myrrh and the hill of frankincense. But she remained there until she was transferred somewhere else. She said that she would go the mountain of myrrh and to the hill of frankincense, but eventually the Lord called her to leave Mount Lebanon. "Come with me from Lebanon, my bride; / With me from Lebanon come" (v. 8). Myrrh signifies the Lord's death, and frankincense signifies the Lord's resurrection, while Lebanon is a type of the Lord's ascension. She said that she would go to the mountain of the Lord's death and the hill of the Lord's resurrection, but eventually she arrived at the top of the Lord's ascension. The experience of the Lord's death and resurrection transferred her to the Lord's ascension. Now she is on the mountaintop of the Lord's ascension.

There is always the danger that we will be satisfied with what we have attained. In chapter 2 there was the discrepancy between her and the Lord due to her satisfaction with her attainment. In chapter 1 she was seeking the Lord, and she found what she was seeking. When she received the enjoyment and the satisfaction, she was content to stay there. But the Lord would not agree for her to stay. That was the cause of a controversy and discrepancy between her and the Lord. The Lord will never be content with any state of our Christian life. We are so easily satisfied with our attainments, but He is not. How wonderful that she attained to the mountaintop of the Lord's ascension! Not only had she experienced so much of the Lord's death and resurrection, but she had attained to the mountaintop of the Lord's ascension.

A FURTHER CALL

At this time the Lord gives her a further call. The Lord calls her to leave the mountaintop of Lebanon, which is the mountaintop of His ascension. To leave the house in chapter 2 is right, but it hardly seems right to leave the mountaintop of ascension. It is not easy to get there; so once there, how could we leave? Not to stay in the house is undoubtedly right, but once we have attained to the mountaintop of the Lord's ascension, it seems that we should stay there. But because this is still only an individualistic attainment, the Lord called her away.

I do not believe that any one of us would want to leave if we had reached such an attainment, but the Lord called her to leave. However, before this time He had never called her His sister or His bride. Only now does He call her by such names. "Come with me from Lebanon, my bride;... / You have ravished my heart, my sister, my bride;... / How beautiful is your love, my sister, my bride!" (vv. 8-10). He called her away from Lebanon to go somewhere else. He called her from the mountaintop of ascension to come back to earth. Without coming down from the mountaintop of ascension, it is impossible to have a garden on earth.

This poetry depicts the Christian in the church life. A garden cannot exist in the heavens. A garden must be on the earth. Not long after the Lord calls her away from the mountaintop of ascension, she is a garden on the earth. "A garden enclosed is my sister, my bride, / A spring shut up, a fountain sealed" (v. 12). This garden is not on the mountaintop; it would be difficult to grow so many spices there. The poetry here shows us that shortly after being on the mountaintop, she is on the earth as a garden.

DEATH AND RESURRECTION

There is only one way to be on the mountaintop of the Lord's ascension, that is, by the mountain of myrrh and the hill of frankincense. We must learn to stay continually in the Lord's death and resurrection. Today many seeking Christians have the wrong concept. They believe that they must fast, weep, pray, and wait on the Lord. In a sense this is good, but we can never force the Lord to help us grow. Growth requires days, months, and even years. To pray for a week is easy; even to fast for a week is easy; but to stay at the mountain of myrrh for five years is not easy. We could all fast and pray for a long time without any sleep, but to stay in the Lord's death and resurrection for a length of time is not easy. Yet there is no other way to get to the mountaintop of the Lord's ascension except by the Lord's death and resurrection.

Calling on the Lord and exercising our spirit are indeed wonderful, but we all must realize that these spiritual practices are only to help us enter into the death and resurrection of the Lord. The more we call on the Lord, the more we should be entering into the death and resurrection of the Lord. It is only through the experiences of the death and resurrection of Jesus that we will be transferred to the mountaintop of the Lord's ascension.

DOWN FROM THE MOUNTAIN

Once we arrive there, however, we cannot stay indefinitely. We would be content to stay, but the Lord would say, "Come with me from Lebanon, my bride; / With me from Lebanon come. / Look from the top of Amana, / From the top of Senir and Hermon, / From the lions' dens, / From the leopards' mountains." By this the Lord is telling us that there are still the lions, the leopards, the enemy, and so many needy ones. We would have the satisfaction, but He would not. We would have the rest, yet He would mention the many hungry and thirsty ones. They do not have any rest and satisfaction. So we must go down from the mountaintop of Lebanon to the valley in order to grow a garden.

THE LORD GROWING OUT

Before the seeking one became a garden, she never grew anything for the Lord. There was much appreciation, enjoyment, and partaking, but she herself never grew anything. In chapter 1 she appreciated the Lord as a bundle of myrrh and as a cluster of henna flowers. Then in chapter 2 she enjoyed the Lord as the apple tree, and she was brought into the house of wine. She greatly appreciated and enjoyed the Lord. In chapter 3 she was even perfumed with myrrh and frankincense; that is, she was permeated and mingled with the Lord. She appreciated the Lord, she enjoyed the Lord, and she was even permeated with the Lord, but she never grew anything for the Lord. It is not until she becomes a garden that she begins to grow something. "A garden enclosed is my sister, my bride,... / Your shoots are an orchard of pomegranates / With choicest fruit; / Henna with spikenard, / Spikenard and saffron; / Calamus and cinnamon, / With all the trees of frankincense; / Myrrh and aloes, / With all the chief spices" (4:12-14).

Before she became a garden, she enjoyed the Lord as the myrrh, the henna flower, and the frankincense. Now she grows what she enjoyed, but it is no longer for her—it is for others. Now the frankincense is not for her satisfaction but for the Lord's satisfaction. The henna flower is not from the Lord for her appreciation, but it is grown out of her for the Lord's appreciation. In the first aspect, everything was for her, but now everything is for the Lord and for others. At first it was something of the Lord getting into her; now it is something of the Lord growing out of her, because all these things have been wrought into her, have permeated her, and have become a part of her.

A CORPORATE BODY

By the time she becomes a garden, it is no longer an individual matter. We can never satisfy others unless we are built up into a corporate Body.

We cannot grow the things we appreciate, enjoy, and with which we are permeated without being fully built up as a garden. This is why we need the second aspect of the Christian life, the corporate Body. This is what the Lord is looking for today. He is not seeking some individually spiritual and mature persons; He is seeking a corporate Body. Christianity has damaged the entire situation. We have all been spoiled by the wrong concepts. This is why we need the eyes of a dove. All the concepts we have received from Christianity need to be changed.

No matter what we received from the past, we must realize that the Christian life is not for the individual. The Christian life is for a corporate Body. Regardless of how high our attainment might be, though it be to the mountaintop of Lebanon, it should never be for ourselves individually. When we arrive there, the Lord will tell us to come down to be a garden on the earth. We cannot stay by ourselves on the mountaintop of ascension. We must go down to the valley to be built up with others and to grow all the things of the Lord with which we have been permeated. We need not only to take in but to grow out. We must be a garden to grow something for the Lord's satisfaction and be a fountain for others.

THE TURNING POINTS

In the next chapter we will see another little discrepancy between this seeking one and the Lord. It is really difficult for us to go on with the Lord all the time. We cannot pursue Him day by day without knowing all the turning points. The Song of Songs is a short book, yet it covers all the turning points of our Christian life.

To be a crown with a tower of David is marvelous, but upon arriving at that stage, we immediately need a turn; we cannot stay. We need a turn from that attainment to the mountain of myrrh and the hill of frankincense. After staying there for a length of time, we need another attainment. Because of the experiences of the Lord's death and resurrection, we will be transferred into His ascension. We will attain to the mountaintop of the Lord's ascension—an attainment higher than the former one. Then we immediately need another turn. From the mountaintop of the Lord's ascension, the Lord will call us away to the valley to be a garden. We cannot be a garden on the mountaintop. We must come down to the valley where we can grow something.

Clearly, a garden is for growing things. When the seeking one becomes a garden, she begins to grow all the things that she has previously enjoyed of the Lord, such as myrrh, frankincense, and henna flowers. All these were the very aspects and items of what the Lord was to her. She enjoyed and partook of all these things, and now she is growing them for the Lord's satisfaction. In the foregoing chapters *she* enjoyed all these things, but in the garden *the Lord Himself* comes in to enjoy them. "I have come into my garden, my sister, my bride; / I have gathered my myrrh with my spice; / I have eaten my honeycomb with my honey; / I have drunk my wine with my milk. / Eat, O friends; / Drink, and drink deeply, O beloved ones!" (5:1).

These are the turning points, and they are also a real exercise in the submission of the will. We should never think we are so spiritual that we have no further need of learning to submit our will. We will need the exercise of the submission of our will until we get to the New Jerusalem.

NEVER BEING CONTENTED

Contentment with our spiritual attainments is a real problem. After arriving at the mountain of myrrh and the hill of frankincense, we are transferred to the mountain of Lebanon, and once there, we want to stay. However, the Lord will never allow us to stay. He will say, "Come with Me to the valley to be a garden." Our individual spiritual attainment is only for ourselves individually. We must leave our attainment with the Lord in order to become a garden for the Lord and for others. This is the way that the garden comes forth. It is not only by the adequate experiences of the Lord's death, resurrection, and ascension, for after we have reached the mountaintop, we must answer the call from the Lord to leave our attainment and return to the place where the Lord intends to fulfill His purpose. We left the valley to go to the mountaintop of ascension; now we must go back to be a garden to grow many things for the Lord's satisfaction. It is only there that the Lord can enjoy Himself out of us. He came into us as our enjoyment, but now we grow Him out for His enjoyment and the enjoyment of others. This is the garden.

We need to see these turning points in order to go on. When the Lord brought Peter, James, and John from the valley to the mountaintop, they saw a real vision of Himself.

Then Peter said, "Lord, it is good for us to be here. Let us build some tabernacles and stay here permanently." But not long after this, the Lord took them from the mountaintop down to the valley. I believe it was after this experience that Peter gradually became a garden.

TURNING ALL THE TIME

We need all these turns in our spiritual life. We need to be turning all the time. Many turns are revealed in this book. To understand all the turns is to understand the book. Following the crown is the turn to the mountain of myrrh and the hill of frankincense. Then this will transfer us to the mountaintop of Lebanon. But immediately we need another turn. We must return to the valley to be a garden. The garden grows the myrrh, the frankincense, the henna flower, and all the other spices. In 3:6 she was permeated with the myrrh and frankincense and all the fragrant powders of the merchant. These powders were simply all the other spices. This indicates that all the things of the Lord of which she partook are now growing out of her. They are not for her enjoyment anymore but for the Lord's enjoyment. The Lord will enjoy Himself grown out of her, and she will be a real supply to others. May the Lord have mercy upon us that we may be willing to turn again and again until we become a garden to fulfill His purpose.

CHAPTER TEN

FROM THE GARDEN TO THE CITY

Scripture Reading: S. S. 5:2-6, 8, 10, 16; 6:1-4; Isa. 53:3-4; Col. 1:24; Phil. 3:10

We have seen that the Song of Songs is clearly divided into two sections. The first section is mainly for the satisfaction and enjoyment of the seeking one. In the first three chapters she appreciates and enjoys the Lord, and she is permeated with the Lord. All the riches of the Lord are for her. By enjoying all these things, she is transformed by steps from a mare to a crown. All the natural things are gone; everything becomes spiritual. In a sense, she attains to the maturity of life, for she is a crown. If we were the writer of this book, we would probably stop here, because the seeking one has reached the utmost attainment of her spiritual life. But this is only the first section, which is for herself.

WORK BY GROWING

The second section is not for her but for the Lord and for others. For this she had to be transferred from a crown to a garden. This involved at least three turns. As a garden she grows all the things that she had enjoyed of the Lord. She enjoyed the Lord as the myrrh, and now she grows myrrh. She enjoyed the Lord as the henna flower, and now she grows the henna flower. She enjoyed the Lord as the frankincense, and now she grows the frankincense. She enjoyed the perfume of all the powders, and now she grows all the spices for making the powders. In the first section the Lord was everything *to* her, but now in the second section the Lord enjoys everything *out of* her. In other words, now the Lord enjoys all that He is through her and out of her.

In today's Christianity, most of the attention is given to the first aspect, that is, individual spirituality. The second aspect is completely neglected. Christians are encouraged to work for God but are not told that the way to work for God is not by the outer working but by the inner growth. When the Lord has been wrought into us, then we will grow out something, and this something will be our working. We do not need to work, but we do need to grow something.

After the seeking one is transferred into the second section, she grows and produces all the items of Christ that she herself has been enjoying. Now her producing is just her work, and her producing becomes satisfaction, contentment, and enjoyment for the Lord Jesus and for all His believers.

LIFE NEEDING DEVELOPMENT

Some would think that all these things are far beyond our experience and therefore are too deep, but I do not believe that this is so. In spiritual matters, it is really difficult to say what is deep and what is not deep. It is not like studying a subject that is learned lesson by lesson. It is a matter of life. A baby has all the elements of human life, but they are not fully developed. Therefore, we should not think that these things are too deep. In a sense, many of us have experienced all these turns already. They simply are not yet fully developed.

I believe that many of us are crowns to the Lord. We are, in a sense, a crown to the Lord in our home, in our school, and at our job. Even the Lord Jesus is satisfied with us. We are Solomon with the crown. But we still need a turn. In spite of our high attainment, there are still some shadows, and our day has not broken. We must get ourselves to the mountain of death and the hill of resurrection and stay there for a length of time. We should not think that this is too deep. We all need such a turn.

Let us open ourselves before the Lord. I do believe we all have the sense that our day has not yet dawned. We all realize that there are still some shadows. No matter how much we say, "Lord Jesus, I love You—You are altogether lovely," there is still the sense that we are not clearly in the day. This is good. As long as we have such a realization, we will

spontaneously say, "Until the day dawns and the shadows
flee away, / I, for my part, will go to the mountain of myrrh /
And to the hill of frankincense" (4:6). We all have such a long-
ing deep within. This is a turn, and this is the Lord moving
and working within us. So we must learn to stay in the Lord's
death and resurrection until the day dawns and all the shadows flee away.

LIFE TAKING TIME

We should not expect this to happen overnight. Some
Christians today are urging people to fast and pray all night.
Years ago, I did much of this. It was our custom during the
last night of every year to stay up all night praying. We ate
nothing that evening and spent all our time dealing with the
Lord. We confessed all our shortcomings, failures, mistakes,
and offenses during the past twelve months, hoping that the
next day would find us absolutely renewed. But it only lasted
about three days. We were still the same. I do not mean that
fasting and praying are not good. Sometimes we need to fast
and pray. The point is that we cannot be changed overnight. I
do not encourage or discourage you to fast. We must go to the
mountain of death and the hill of resurrection and stay there.
Life takes time.

Many times we are desperate with the Lord, but the Lord
says, "I am resting." We tell the Lord that we are going to fast
and pray for three days, but the Lord says, "Take something
to eat and go to sleep." Many of us have experienced this. We
should not trust in our fasting and praying all night. We must
learn to stay at the mountain of myrrh and the hill of frankincense. We must remain in the Lord's death and resurrection
for a length of time.

In the New Testament, especially in the Epistles, we
cannot find many verses to support the teaching concerning
fasting that we hear in today's Christianity. On the other
hand, the apostle Paul tells us many times how we must experience the Lord's death. He repeatedly mentions this principle,
as in Philippians 3:10: "To know Him and the power of His
resurrection and the fellowship of His sufferings, being conformed to His death." Paul does not speak of experiencing a

portion of the Lord's death but of staying there until we will be "conformed to His death." We will be continually tested and proved by our families, our surroundings, and our circumstances. All these things will test us to see if we are remaining in the Lord's death and resurrection.

A SPONTANEOUS TURN

If we learn to stay in the Lord's death and resurrection, we will be transferred into His ascension. The mountain of myrrh and the hill of frankincense always transfer us to the mountaintop of Lebanon. If we take this turn, the next turn will occur spontaneously. The Lord's death and resurrection will always carry us to His ascension. We expect to stay at the mountain of myrrh and the hill of frankincense, but we find ourselves on the mountaintop of Lebanon. Here we are content and satisfied. We never want to leave. This is the Lord's ascension! We would stay here for eternity. We were a crown, but we have now soared to the highest attainment, to be in the Lord's ascension.

But the Lord Jesus is still not satisfied. This is still only something for us; it is not so much for Him. We have attained to the highest, but God's purpose has still not been fulfilled. This is why the Lord calls the seeking one to leave the mountain of ascension and to behold the situation on earth. Many are still hungry and thirsty, and the enemy is still causing much trouble. Even the Lord Himself is hungry and thirsty. He has nothing to enjoy. So she must become a garden to grow all the things that she has enjoyed of the Lord. All the items that she has enjoyed of the Lord must now grow out of her for the enjoyment of the Lord and for so many of the Lord's believers.

Our destination is not to stay on the mountaintop of ascension but to come down to the valley to be a garden to grow all the things to fulfill God's eternal purpose. It is through the garden that a city can be built up.

Many turning points occur in this book. From the crown there is a turn to the mountain of myrrh and the hill of frankincense. Then, spontaneously, the death and resurrection of the Lord send us to the mountaintop of ascension. But then the Lord calls us to have another turn to come down and be a garden. To understand this book is to understand all the turning points. My burden is simply to point out all the turning points so that we may know the way to go. When we are driving in unfamiliar territory, we need a map. If we have a proper map, then we know where to turn in order to go on. All the turning points in this book show us how we can progress in our spiritual life.

ANOTHER DISCREPANCY

Now the seeking one has answered the Lord's call to come down to the valley to become a garden. But she is still not yet a city. In a sense, the garden is close to the city; yet when we consider the Bible, the garden is far removed from the city. The garden is at the beginning of the sixty-six books, and the city is at the end. She is now a garden, growing out the things she once enjoyed of the Lord; however, even in being a garden, some kind of discrepancy between her and the Lord still exists. "I sleep, but my heart is awake. / A sound! My beloved is knocking. / Open to me, my sister, my love, / My dove, my perfect one; / For my head is drenched with dew, / My locks with the drops of night. / I have put off my garment; / How can I put it on again? / I have washed my feet; / How can I dirty them again?" (S. S. 5:2-3).

We have seen the discrepancy between the Lord and the seeking one in chapter 2. But as we read the record in chapter 5, it seems nearly the same. In chapter 2 she was in the house, and the Lord was outside the wall. Now, the Lord is satisfied with her as a garden, and she is content and happy. She even declares that her outward man is dead, for she declares that she sleeps outwardly. She has retired from all her activities. Yet inwardly she is awakened. She says, "I sleep, but my heart is awake." This poetry indicates that while she is so content, she suddenly hears the voice of the Lord. This means that she realizes the Lord is not with her. Again she is inside, and the Lord is outside.

A DEEPER EXPERIENCE OF THE CROSS

What is the reason for this discrepancy? It seems that she

did nothing wrong. She is now a garden for the Lord's enjoyment—why is there still some discrepancy? In our earlier
years, we spent much time trying to understand this point. It
was not until 1935, when Brother Nee was going through this
book with a few of us, that this point became clear. It was
then the Lord showed us that this was a deeper experience of
the cross. The Lord said, "My head is drenched with dew, / My
locks with the drops of night." What He means is that while
the seeking one is content and satisfied. He is suffering. Such
a picture in poetry depicts the suffering Christ. He is also
shown in this manner in Isaiah 53:3-4. "He was despised and
forsaken of men, / A man of sorrows, and acquainted with
grief; / And like one from whom men hide their faces, / He was
despised; and we did not esteem Him. / Surely He has borne
our sicknesses, / And carried our sorrows; / Yet we ourselves
esteemed Him stricken, / Smitten of God and afflicted."

He is really the man of sorrows. Especially at the garden
of Gethsemane, He was under the dew of the night. The
Lord's words to the seeking one reveal Himself as such a suffering One. He is "a man of sorrows and acquainted with
grief." And now He is calling her to be such a suffering one
with Him.

Before the Lord became man, He was in the heavenlies.
Then the time came for Him to be incarnated, and He put on
our human nature as a kind of cloak. He became the "man of
sorrows," and He was suffering under the dew of the night.

Now the seeking one is in the heavenlies, and the Lord
calls her to come down out of the heavenlies to put on something to suffer for Him. But she tells the Lord, "I have put off
my garment; / How can I put it on again? / I have washed my
feet; / How can I dirty them again?" In other words, she is
saying, "I have put off the old nature. I am in the heavenlies;
therefore, how can I put it on again?"

FILLING UP THE AFFLICTIONS OF CHRIST

I realize that this point is not so easy to understand, but
we must see it very clearly. For the seeking ones of the Lord
to deny the world is a marvelous thing; to deny themselves is
even more glorious. But one day the Lord will call us to deny

our spiritual attainment, even as He did. He was the very God, but in a sense He put His divinity aside to come down to earth to be a man (Phil. 2:5-8). By becoming a man, He denied what He was as God; yet He still was God. He became not a glorious man but a man of low estate. He sacrificed all that He was in order to come to the earth to accomplish God's purpose by suffering as a "man of sorrows."

Perhaps we also have reached a high attainment. We are now so spiritual and heavenly. This is sufficient for us, but it is not sufficient for the Lord's purpose. So in a sense, we must deny our spiritual attainment to come down and take a low estate with the Lord.

Paul the apostle did many things that caused the religious people to misunderstand him. It seems that he relinquished all his attainment to fill up the lack of the afflictions of Christ. He speaks of this in Colossians 1:24: "I now rejoice in my sufferings on your behalf and fill up on my part that which is lacking of the afflictions of Christ in my flesh for His Body, which is the church." We have no share in the Lord's suffering for redemption—only the Lord could suffer for our redemption. But we can suffer for the building up of the Body. We need to fill up the lack of the Lord's affliction for His Body's sake. Many times people thought that Paul was rejected by God, but he was suffering for the Body of Christ.

Today, in principle, it is exactly the same. So many Christians in Christianity are seeking spirituality in a general way. But after they reach the highest attainment of spirituality, if they really mean business with the Lord, the Lord will call them to deny their spirituality for the eternal purpose of God. Many so-called spiritual Christians would not offend anyone. They like to keep themselves continually in the heavenlies—so high, so wonderful, so spiritual—like angels. But the Lord will say, "Let us leave Lebanon and go down into the valley. I am the suffering One under the dew, and there is still a lack in My suffering which needs to be filled. You are spiritual, and everyone admires you, but where is My Body? Where is My church?"

If we stay in the heavenlies, we will be spiritual and never offend anyone. We will be gentle and nice to all and never get ourselves involved with others. But what about God's purpose? I have been warned many times by dear friends not to mention the church. Then everyone would be happy with me, and all the groups would invite me to come and speak to them. They have told me that I should not be so much for the church, that this will only create many enemies, and I will just sacrifice myself.

The Song of Songs makes it very clear that if we only care for the Lord's eternal purpose and not for our spirituality, we will be a man of sorrows. Not only the world but also Christianity will persecute us. Even many spiritual Christians will persecute us. But we must open ourselves to the One who is under the dew and the drops of night. This is the filling up of the lack of Christ's suffering for His Body.

SICK WITH LOVE

The seeking one who reached such high attainment in her spiritual life still has some discrepancy between her and the Lord. She is much with the Lord, yet there is still some unwillingness. He calls her, and she hesitates. She gives the Lord a very good excuse. She says, "I have put off my old way of being. How can I put it on again? I have washed my feet from the dirt of the earth. How can I defile them again?" These are good excuses, but when the Lord calls, He does not care how good the excuses are.

At this point, she realizes that the Lord is gone. "I opened to my beloved, / But my beloved had withdrawn; he was gone. / My soul failed when he spoke; / I sought him, but found him not; / I called him—he answered me not... / I adjure you, O daughters of Jerusalem, / If you find my beloved, / What shall you tell him? / That I am sick with love" (5:6, 8). She seeks the Lord, but she cannot find Him. She calls, but the Lord does not answer her. Others try to help her, and she tells them that she is sick with love for the Lord.

She is asked by all the others, "Where is your beloved gone, / O you most beautiful among women? / Where has your beloved turned, / That we may seek him with you?" (6:1). While she is telling them about the Lord, she realizes that the Lord has not left; He is still in His garden. "My beloved has gone down to his garden, / To the beds of spices, / To feed in the gardens / And gather lilies. / I am my beloved's, and my beloved is mine; / He pastures his flock among the lilies" (vv. 2-3).

We all have had this kind of experience. Sometimes we feel that the Lord is gone, and we begin to talk to others about Him. But while we are talking, we realize that the Lord is still with us. We thought He was far away, but He is still in His garden, pasturing His flock among the lilies. He is still in us, and we are His, and He is ours.

A DEEPER TURN

At this time a further and deeper transforming work is done in the seeking one. Now the Lord says to her, "You are as beautiful, my love, as Tirzah, / As lovely as Jerusalem, / As terrible as an army with banners" (v. 4). After the turn in chapter 4, the Lord likens her to a garden. But after this deeper turn, the Lord likens her to a city.

I do not believe that any other teachings or instructions could help us in our spiritual growth as much as all these points. We do not need to learn this book in a way of knowledge, but we must see all the turning points for our spiritual growth that this book opens up. We need to fellowship and pray over these points many times. All these lessons will be repeated again and again in a kind of cycle as we go on with the Lord. By all the cycles we will grow from the crown to the garden, and then from the garden to the city and the army. This is the way for us to fulfill God's eternal purpose and to build up the Body of Christ.

CHAPTER ELEVEN

PRODUCING THE BODY OF CHRIST

Scripture Reading: S. S. 5:2-6, 8, 16; 6:1-6; Phil. 3:10; Col. 1:24

The Song of Songs is really a wonderful book. Again we must say that our intention is not merely to understand this book. That means nothing. What we must see are all the turning points in life so that we may grow up for God's eternal purpose, the corporate building. Our main emphasis in all these messages is life and building. Life is for building, and building issues out of life. We must see the turns in life to have the maturity. The maturity in life will then produce the building.

Though we have no intention to merely understand this book, we still need to be familiar with all the terms, expressions, illustrations, and figures. This is a poetic writing, and in such a writing, these figures are important. We are not for the mere knowledge of the Bible, but we are for knowing all the turns in life. Therefore, I feel that we need a review of all the figures we have covered thus far.

SEEKING THE LORD

This book shows us that the spiritual growth in life begins with seeking the Lord. Our seeking is always the result of our being attracted and drawn by the Lord. Whenever the Lord shows Himself to us, spontaneously we will be drawn to seek after Him. The seeking in this book is in a way of love. When we are attracted by the Lord, we start to seek Him by loving Him. After the seeking, there is the finding, which brings us into the real fellowship with the Lord. The seeking brings the finding, and the finding brings the fellowship.

In the first chapter of this book, the seeking one was brought into the inner chamber of the King. She was even sitting at the King's table. This indicates an intimate and intensified fellowship with the Lord. It is by fellowship with the Lord that we begin to appreciate Him. The first step in our experience is not to enjoy the Lord directly but to appreciate Him. Here the seeking one began to appreciate the Lord as a bundle of myrrh and a cluster of henna flowers. These were all appreciations of the Lord. She truly appreciated His sweetness, His fairness, and His beauty.

In the last verse of chapter 1, she entered into a further and deeper fellowship with the Lord: "The beams of our house are cedars; / Our rafters are cypresses." The cedar signifies resurrection, and the rafters of cypresses signify the death of Christ. By this she came into a closer fellowship with the Lord.

TRANSFORMATION BEGINS

By all these appreciations of the Lord she entered into the first step of transformation. She was likened by the Lord to a mare among Pharaoh's chariots. She still had her natural strength, and she was carrying something worldly. But gradually her eyes were changed to doves' eyes. Then, her concept was radically changed by more appreciation of the Lord. The more we appreciate the Lord's sweetness and fairness, the more our mind will be renewed. We will lose the view of our natural birth and begin to have the insight of the Spirit.

By the closer and deeper fellowship with the Lord mentioned in the last verse of chapter 1, she became a lily trusting only in God. A mare is full of its own strength, but a lily has no strength in which to trust. The natural strength was lost; she realized that to go on with the Lord she must drop all her natural power to do things for Him. She began to put her trust in God; this is the living of the lily. She became even as one of the little lilies growing in the field, trusting in God's care. She did not live by her own labor and toil but by trusting in God. This is real transformation.

FROM APPRECIATION TO ENJOYMENT

After the seeking one became a lily, she began to enjoy the Lord. At first, she appreciated the Lord as a bundle of myrrh and as a cluster of henna flowers, but at that time she had not yet begun to enjoy the Lord. The enjoyment began after she was transformed into a lily. After becoming a lily, she started to enjoy the Lord's fruit, which was sweet to her taste. Then, she not only appreciated the Lord but also enjoyed the Lord by eating of His fruit. After this, she was brought into the banqueting house, the house of wine, to have a further enjoyment of eating and drinking the Lord. Before that time, she only had a kind of appreciation of the Lord. The riches of the Lord had not yet been deposited into her. But when she started to enjoy the Lord, she began to take something of the Lord into her. By eating and drinking of the Lord, some of the elements of the Lord were wrought into her. Hence, by eating, drinking, and enjoying the Lord, the third step of transformation was wrought into the seeking one. She became a dove. A dove in the Bible signifies the Holy Spirit. As a dove, she lived as the Spirit, behaved as the Spirit, and had the appearance of the Spirit. As a dove, she became the expression of the Spirit. It was not only by appreciating the Lord but by taking the Lord Himself into her in a way of enjoyment that some of the Lord's very element entered into her and caused her to be transformed substantially. She was no longer a mare or a lily but a dove, the expression of the life-giving Spirit.

PARTICIPATING IN THE LORD'S DEATH AND RESURRECTION

All her transformation was due to her appreciation and enjoyment of the Lord through the experiences of the Lord's death and resurrection. Many figures, such as the myrrh, the clefts of the rock, and the covert of the precipice are pictures of the Lord's death and resurrection. While she was appreciating and enjoying the Lord, she experienced the Lord's death and resurrection. We cannot partake of the Lord Himself without participating in His death and resurrection, because these are elements of His very being. If we enjoy Him, surely we will participate in His death and resurrection. The more we partake of the Lord, the more we take His death into us. The more we enjoy Him, the more we take in His resurrection.

The Lord today is just like an all-inclusive dose. In such a dose are all the ingredients and elements that are needed. There are the killing elements, and there are the nourishing elements. The Lord's death is the killing element, and His resurrection is the nourishing element. When we enjoy the Lord, we enjoy all the ingredients of such an all-inclusive One. The more we take the Lord in, the more the killing elements get into us. At the same time, we also obtain the nourishing elements of His resurrection. Hallelujah! As the Lord's element gets into us, He kills all the negative items and nourishes us with all the positive elements. This results in transformation. The mare's eyes were changed into doves' eyes, and even the mare was changed into a lily. Then the lily was transformed into a dove, and she stayed in the clefts of the rock and in the covert of the precipice. She stayed in the Lord's death, resurrection, and ascension.

NO PERSONALITY

Then she came out of her spiritual wilderness, which was just her will. She came out like pillars of smoke, perfumed with myrrh and frankincense and all the fragrant powders of the merchant. In the foregoing pictures, she had some kind of personality, but now as pillars she has no personality. She was dealt with by the Lord to such an extent that her personality was gone.

In our spiritual life, the problem is always with our personality. Every person has a strong personality. Dealing with things is no problem, because things have no personality. But dealing with people is always a problem because of the differences in personality. The Lord must deal with our personality because it conflicts with His. In the last four figures of the first group, however, there was no personality. The seeking one had come out of her will, and her personality had been thoroughly dealt with. There was no personality in the pillars, the bed, the palanquin, or the crown. Hallelujah!

Eight figures constitute the first group: the mare, the

doves' eyes, the lily, the dove, the pillars, the bed, the palanquin, and the crown. Between the first four figures, many things occur. The appreciation and the enjoyment of the Lord Jesus cause transformation from one figure to the next. But between the last four figures nothing seems to be taking place. The pillars, the bed, the palanquin, and the crown all seem to be alike. Once we attain to the stage of losing our personality, we will be all four of these figures at the same time.

Who then is our personality? Hallelujah! We can see this clearly in the figure of the palanquin. The palanquin itself has no personality, but within the palanquin there is a person. This person is the personality of the palanquin. His will is the palanquin's will. His emotion is the palanquin's emotion. His mind is the palanquin's mind. The palanquin itself does not have any personality, but it contains the living person of the King within it. These figures speak more to us than a number of messages on how to be spiritual. If we simply look at these pictures, we are clear. When we come out of the wilderness of our will, we become the pillars, the bed, the palanquin, and the crown. We become the Lord's boast and glory, and He becomes our full and complete personality.

In the beginning, the seeking one's emotion was touched by the Lord (1:2-4). Then gradually, her mind was renewed (v. 15). Eventually, her will was subdued (3:6). Her whole being was transformed. She became so one with the Lord within, that she became the outward expression of the Lord. This was seen in both the palanquin and the crown. The Lord was in the palanquin, and He was under the crown. Therefore, she was described as being Solomon with the crown. The two became one. This was really the highest attainment of spirituality.

THREE MAIN TURNS

However, that is only the first half of the book, showing only the first half of the poetic portrayal of our spiritual experiences. At that point she still needed the mountain of myrrh and the hill of frankincense. This means that even with such a high attainment, her day had not yet dawned; some shadows still existed. She was not content with what she had attained. She realized that she needed more of the Lord's death and resurrection; she must stay there. By staying at the mountain of myrrh and the hill of frankincense, she was transferred to the mountaintop of Lebanon, which is the mountaintop of the Lord's ascension. This is always true whenever we experience the Lord's death and resurrection.

To be transformed into the palanquin and the crown is a high attainment, yet the peak of the mountaintop of the Lord's ascension is even higher. But then the Lord came to call her to the next turn. The first turn was mostly made by herself. She realized that she needed the mountain of myrrh and the hill of frankincense, and the second turn was made by the experience of the Lord's death and resurrection. Then the Lord came to help her make the third turn. He called her to leave her highest attainment, to leave the mountaintop of Lebanon, and to go down to the valley to be a garden.

A PRODUCING GARDEN

By this time she had enjoyed the Lord richly, but she had never produced anything for the Lord's enjoyment. She had satisfaction, but she had not produced anything for the Lord and for others. She must become a garden to grow out something for the Lord and for His people. Hence, she did become a garden producing all the things she enjoyed of the Lord in the past. She enjoyed myrrh; now she grows myrrh. She enjoyed frankincense and the henna flower; now she grows frankincense and the henna flower. She enjoyed all of the fragrant powders of the merchant; now she grows all the spices for making the powders. Whatever she had enjoyed, she now grows. In her enjoyment the Lord entered into her, and now in her growth the Lord comes out of her. The Lord firstly wrought Himself into her, and now He is producing Himself out of her.

This is not mere doctrine; it is the real experience of the spiritual life. So many will tell you that this is exactly what they have been experiencing of the Lord. We all must be such a garden to the Lord, growing out all that we have enjoyed of Him. On the day we were saved, we became, in a sense, a garden, producing something for the Lord and for others. But that was not so adequate. We have to grow, step by step, stage by stage, until we reach the stage of being a garden. In a sense we have been a garden, but we are not in the stage of a garden. We must go on until we arrive at the stage of being a garden.

A FURTHER DISCREPANCY

After the seeking one reached the stage of a garden, according to the poetry, she became contented again. She was so satisfied with her spiritual attainment that it created a kind of discrepancy between her and the Lord. Every time we are contented with our spiritual attainment, this satisfaction becomes a discrepancy between us and the Lord. We are satisfied, but the Lord would have us go on. We must not stay with what we have attained. It is wonderful to be a crown, but do not stay there. It is marvelous to be on the top of Lebanon, but do not stay there. It is splendid to come down and become a garden, but do not stay there. Once we are content, we lose the presence of the Lord.

OUTWARDLY SLEEPING, INWARDLY LIVING

Because of her contentment, the seeking one has a repetition of the experience in chapter 2. She is within, and He is without. But this time the situation is much different. She says, "I sleep, but my heart is awake." This is a fact; by this time she is really resting from all her activity. This is a real improvement in her spiritual life. We are always wanting to do too many things. But the more we grow in the Lord, the more we give up natural activity; we rest from all our activities. Outwardly we sleep, but inwardly we are living! We are very much on the alert for the Lord's presence and for His voice. We can hear the Lord immediately whenever He speaks, and we can realize whether His presence is with us or not. It is by this that she discovers a discrepancy between her and the Lord.

When we are away from the Lord, He will always call us back to Him. When we come back to Him, we become exceedingly active to do many things for Him. But gradually, especially as we get into the church life, all our activities will be slain. Eventually, we will simply say, "I sleep." There are no more activities. But we are not dead! We are very living within!

Many times those outside of the church condemn us by saying that the church life stops many good activities. So many missionaries, after contacting the church, ceased going to the mission field. All the denominations encourage Christians to go to the mission field. But the proper church life stops them from going. This is true. So many missionaries, pastors, and Christian workers have become captured by the church life from all their natural activities. The more we stay in the church, the more we are dead to our activity. Then we rest from all our activities outwardly. But inwardly we are exceedingly living, always listening for the voice of the Lord.

When we are active, the Lord will tell us to be quiet. But when we become quiet, resting from all our activities, the Lord will say, "Don't be so quiet. I'm still under the dew and the drops of night." He is still working and suffering to fulfill God's purpose. In a sense, He has accomplished everything and has ascended to the heavens where He sits at the right hand of God. But in another sense, He is still working and suffering to build His corporate Body. The Lord shows the seeking one that while she is resting, He is still working. This reveals to her the discrepancy between her and the Lord.

This is a real picture of the incarnation. The Lord was God, but He became a man. As God, it was not necessary for Him to be under the dew to suffer in the night. But He became a "man of sorrows," continually suffering for God's purpose. The Lord was asking her to relinquish all her spiritual attainment and to suffer with Him for God's purpose. Her reply was, "I have put off my garment; / How can I put it on again? / I have washed my feet; / How can I dirty them again?" This poetry shows how she had put off all her natural life and washed away all her defilements from the world. She was so spiritual, so undefiled, so pure, and so holy. How could she go back?

THE FELLOWSHIP OF HIS SUFFERINGS

Paul said in Philippians 3:10 that he wanted to know the

fellowship of the sufferings of Christ. This means that Paul desired participation in His sufferings. If the Lord had stayed in the heavens, He would never have been a man who suffered on the earth. Then it would have been impossible to produce the church, the Body of Christ. The Body is produced through the sufferings of Christ. Christ suffered not only for our redemption but also for the producing of the Body. But the producing of the Body has not yet been completed. There is a lack in the afflictions of Christ. Therefore Paul said, "I now rejoice in my sufferings on your behalf and fill up on my part that which is lacking of the afflictions of Christ in my flesh for His Body, which is the church" (Col. 1:24). Paul filled up the lack of the afflictions of Christ for the Body's sake. But do not think that the Body of Christ has been completed. Even today, we must complete the Body by suffering the same kind of afflictions the Lord Jesus suffered as a man.

Paul was very religious before he was saved. Then he was saved and became so spiritual. I would say that he even reached the highest attainment of spirituality. But he did not stay there. Apparently, he lost all his spirituality to suffer for the Body of Christ. Today there are many so-called servants of the Lord who have never touched any secular job or worldly business. Once they begin to serve the Lord, they would never go back to any kind of business. But have you realized that Paul was in the tentmaking business even after he reached such a high attainment of spirituality? He was not making tents for his own use. He was making them to sell to others. Paul might have received criticism for this, which would have been a suffering to him. After reaching such a high attainment in spirituality, he continued to make and sell tents! But he was filling up the lack of the afflictions of Christ for His Body's sake.

SUFFERING TO PRODUCE THE BODY

We cannot participate in Christ's suffering for redemption. But we must take part in the sufferings of Christ for the producing of the Body. Consider further the situation of the apostle Paul. He was a Pharisee in the Jewish religion, a position highly respected and honored by many people. But he left it and became a Christian. Moreover, he attained to the mountaintop of spirituality. Not only were the Judaizers not building up the Body of Christ, but also many so-called Christian workers were not doing the proper things to produce and build the Body of Christ. Paul was the only one in the Gentile world willing to suffer for the Lord's Body. He was criticized and opposed; some even tried to kill him. He suffered these things to fill up the lack of Christ's afflictions for His Body's sake.

Now let us look at today's situation. Christianity is just like Judaism. It is respected and honored, yet it does not care for the Body of Christ. Many so-called free preachers have left the denominations, but they only care for their own ministry; they care little for the Body of Christ. Hence, they do not suffer for the sake of the Body.

Because the Lord has burdened us for the Body, we cannot avoid suffering. We are forced to take a special standing, a standing which is absolutely different from Christianity and the free groups. Of course, this causes much criticism and opposition to come to us. But this is the suffering for producing the Body.

We may think that we love the Lord, but when we begin to suffer for His Body's sake, the love between us and the Lord will become exceedingly sweet. We will be sick with love, and we will tell others that our Lord Jesus is altogether lovely. We will realize more of His love and more of His loveliness. We will learn that no matter how we feel, the Lord is always within us. Whether we sense His presence or not, He is still there. Through these experiences, we will become a city as God's dwelling place, God's habitation, and also an army to stand against God's enemy. This will be the fulfillment of God's purpose in us.

CHAPTER TWELVE

THE DANCE OF TWO CAMPS

Scripture Reading: S. S. 5:4-6, 8-9, 16; 6:1-6, 10, 13

FOUR ATTAINMENTS

As we have seen in the past chapters, the seeking one in the Song of Songs reached at least four attainments. In chapter 2 she reached the first attainment, after which she became contented. Due to this, a discrepancy arose between her and the Lord. The second attainment was reached when she became a crown to the Lord. Yet at that time she herself realized that there were still some shadows and that her day had not yet dawned. Hence, she progressed by going to the mountain of myrrh and the hill of frankincense. By this she was transferred to the top of Lebanon. This was her third attainment, at which she again became contented. The Lord then came to call her from what she had attained. She answered the Lord's call to reach the fourth attainment by becoming a garden. This is a much further, higher, and deeper attainment. Formerly, she was enjoying the Lord, but now she is producing the Lord. She was a partaker, but now she has become a producer. The poetry here reveals that she now becomes very contented, even more contented than she was in chapter 2. Therefore, she says, "I sleep, but my heart is awake." At this juncture the Lord calls her again to leave her attainment.

Thus, we see four attainments in chapters 2 through 5, with at least one in each chapter. The last attainment was reached when she became a producing garden, growing out what she had enjoyed of the Lord. But still the Lord's purpose

had not been accomplished. The garden is not the consummation of the Bible; it is only the beginning.

TWO MAIN DISCREPANCIES

In these four attainments, we see two main discrepancies
between her and the Lord. The first is in chapter 2, and the
second is in chapter 5. These two discrepancies really speak
something to us. I must say again, this is not a book of teaching but a map for our spiritual driving. It reveals all the turns
we must make in order to fulfill God's eternal purpose.

In the discrepancy of chapter 2, she heard the voice of the
Lord, and she saw the Lord's countenance. But in the discrepancy of chapter 5, the Lord showed her His hand: "My beloved
put his hand into the opening of the door, / And my inner
parts yearned for him" (v. 4). When the Lord showed her His
countenance, He attracted her by His loveliness and His
beauty. His face signifies His beauty. But in the second discrepancy, the Lord did not show her His face but rather His
hand. In the Bible, the hand signifies working and doing.

THE LORD'S WAY OF WORKING

What was the Lord showing her by this vision? He had
already shown her that He was the One under the dew in the
night, suffering for God's purpose. Now He continued by
showing her that whatever He did on this earth was not
according to His own taste, opinion, or feeling. It was absolutely according to the Father's will. He worked for the
Father, not according to His own desire but according to His
Father's desire and to fulfill His Father's purpose. Now it is
not a matter of the Lord's beauty or attractiveness but a
matter of the Lord's working. By this vision the Lord taught
her to take His way of working. If she is to work with Him on
this earth, she must learn to work according to the Lord's
way.

THE SWEET SMELL OF MYRRH

When she saw the Lord's hand, she stretched out her
hands. "I rose up to open to my beloved; / And my hands
dripped with myrrh, / My fingers with liquid myrrh, / Upon

the handles of the bolt" (v. 5). She saw the hand of the Lord, and she replied with her hands dripping with myrrh. In chapter 1 she appreciated the myrrh. In chapter 3 she was perfumed and permeated with myrrh. In chapter 4 there was the mountain of myrrh. Now in chapter 5 her hands are dripping with myrrh. She has become so thoroughly saturated with myrrh that her hands are dripping with myrrh. This signifies that now her work and her doing have been dealt with by the death of Christ. Even in her work, there is the sweet smell of the Lord's death. Her hands give the sense of the cross.

To work for the Lord by going to the mission field or preaching the gospel is one thing, but to work for the Lord with the sweet smell of myrrh is quite another. I may preach the gospel but with no smell of myrrh. I may do much in the name of service for the Lord, yet without the smell of the Lord's death in my work. But after becoming permeated and saturated with the Lord's death, my hands will drip with myrrh. Then I may still preach the gospel, but there will be the sense that this is not just preaching. This is the dripping of the sweet-smelling myrrh.

In poetry, every sentence, every term, every expression, and even every word speaks much. Her hands dripping with myrrh show that all her working for the Lord is under the dealing of the Lord's death. This dealing of death becomes the sweet-smelling myrrh dripping from her working hands. Drops of myrrh even hit the handles of the bolt. This is full of meaning. The door was locked but becomes unlocked by the dripping of the myrrh. There had been a separation between her and the Lord, but the barrier was removed by the myrrh dripping from her hands. In her working, in her doing, in whatever she does for the Lord, there is now the sweet smell of the dripping myrrh.

We all must be like this in our work for the Lord. When we go to visit others for fellowship, is there the dripping of the sweet-smelling myrrh? We may do a lot of visiting, but it means nothing if it is a visitation without the dripping of myrrh. When some visit others, it is not just a mere visitation. Along with the visitation there is the dripping of the sweet-smelling myrrh. The sweet smell of the dealing of the Lord's death is in whatever they do.

FAITH, NOT FEELING

The Lord also taught the seeking one another lesson. During all that time, she had been dealing with the Lord more or less according to her feeling of the Lord's presence. Now the Lord hides His presence from her feeling. She says she opens herself to the Lord and seeks the Lord, but she simply cannot find Him. She calls, but He will not answer her. Has the Lord left her? No, He has not left, but to her sensation and feeling He is gone. Her fellowship with the Lord in the past had been according to her feeling of the Lord's presence. Now the Lord is teaching her not to deal with Him only by her feelings. Whether she feels the Lord's presence or not, He is always there.

Because she cannot find the Lord, she begins to ask others to help her find Him. Then the others ask her about the difference between her beloved and another beloved. As she begins to tell them how altogether lovely her beloved is, she begins to realize that He has never left her. He is within His garden. Now she realizes that whether or not she feels that He is with her, He is, nonetheless, always with her. By this lesson, she learns not to discern the Lord's presence simply by her feeling.

When we lose the feeling of the Lord's presence, the best way to bring it back is to talk with others about Him. This is the experience of the seeking one. As we begin to talk with others about the Lord, we immediately sense that He is with us. We realize that He is in His garden. Not only is He in us, but He is in all His gardens—not only one garden but many gardens. "My beloved has gone down to his garden, / To the beds of spices, / To feed in the gardens / And gather lilies" (6:2). He is feeding and shepherding in all His gardens, and He is feeding among the lilies.

This is very meaningful. We should learn never to care for our feeling of the Lord's presence. Whether we feel that the Lord is with us or not, the Lord is still with us. He is always within us feeding, gathering, and shepherding His garden.

FURTHER TRANSFORMATION

Now the seeking one says, "I am my beloved's, and my beloved is mine; / He pastures his flock among the lilies"(v. 3). Formerly, she said, "My beloved is mine." But now she says, "I am my beloved's." It is not so much that the Lord is for me as it is that I am for the Lord. This shows more growth in life, more improvement, and further transformation. Now she is like the apostle Paul, suffering for the Lord's purpose, not working according to her taste but according to God's desire. She is no longer laboring for her contentment or satisfaction but for the fulfilling of God's eternal purpose to build up the Body of Christ. To do this, she surely must take the way of suffering. Just as Paul suffered to fill up the lack of the afflictions of Christ for His Body's sake, this one knows the Lord with the power of His resurrection and the fellowship of His sufferings. She is now being conformed to the death of Christ. Such a one, like Paul, is a useful vessel for God's purpose.

She has lost her will, her personality, and her way to work. All these things have been fully dealt with by the Lord's death. Now she is absolutely one with the Lord for the fulfillment of God's eternal purpose. For this reason the Lord likens her to a city. "You are as beautiful, my love, as Tirzah, / As lovely as Jerusalem, / As terrible as an army with banners" (v. 4). The real consummation of the spiritual life is not her individual, personal satisfaction but the fulfillment of the Lord's eternal purpose to build up His Body. Even chapter 5 shows some personal satisfaction and contentment, but now as a city she is absolutely not for herself. Now she is wholly for God's purpose of building up the church, which is seen at the end of the Bible as a built-up city.

SPIRITUAL SIGHT, SUBMISSION,
AND RECEIVING ABILITY

Now the Lord appraises her again. "Turn your eyes away from me, / For they overwhelm me, / Your hair is like a flock of goats / That repose on Mount Gilead. / Your teeth are like a flock of ewes / That have come up from the washing, / All of which have borne twins, / And none of them is bereaved of her young" (vv. 5-6). Here the Lord mentions mainly three things: her eyes, her hair, and her teeth. The eyes signify the renewing of the mind, the hair signifies the submission and subduing of the will, and the teeth signify the ability to take in or receive food. We cannot take in food properly without teeth. She has learned to feed upon the Lord Jesus.

How she has captured the Lord! Her eyes have overwhelmed Him. Her sight is very spiritual, so much like the dove. It seems that the Lord simply cannot resist her eyes. Her hair, the subduing and submission of her will, is such a beauty to the Lord. Her teeth have such receiving power. All the time she eats of the Lord and takes Him in. These are the three main points of the Lord's appraisal of such a seeking one. We need spiritual sight, we need submission, and we need receiving ability. Through these we will be transformed and changed into a city.

THE DAWN, THE MOON, THE SUN, AND THE ARMY

Now the day dawns, and the shadows really flee away. The Lord likens her to three shining things and one terrifying thing: the dawn, the moon, the sun, and the army. "Who is this woman who looks forth like the dawn, / As beautiful as the moon, / As clear as the sun, / As terrible as an army with banners?" (v. 10). She looks forth like the dawn, the breaking of day. Proverbs 4:18 says, "The path of the righteous is like the light of dawn, / Which shines brighter and brighter until the full day." Now her day really dawns. She herself is just like the dawn. Moreover, she is the moon and the sun. There is no more shadow, no more darkness; she is completely filled with light. As the moon and the sun, she is the light-bearer, full of light.

This is not another stage but is included in the city. These last four figures: the army, the dawn, the moon, and the sun are all included in the city. When she was a garden, she was not yet an army. Now, as the city, she is the army, the dawn, the moon, and the sun. To the Lord she is the city; to the enemy she is the army; and to the whole universe she is the shining one, shining forth all the time. According to the Bible, the sun signifies Christ, and the moon as the reflection of the sun signifies the church. Now she is both Christ and the church; she is both the sun and the moon. This is marvelous! To God she is the city, to Satan she is the army, and to the whole universe she is the sun and the moon. She is shining more and more until the full day.

CONSISTENT VICTORY

Eventually, some of her admirers ask her to return: "Return, return, O Shulammite; / Return, return, that we may gaze at you. / Why should you gaze at the Shulammite, / As upon the dance of two camps?" (S. S. 6:13). It is at this time that her name is called Shulammite. This is the feminine form of *Solomon.* So now she simply becomes Solomon. They ask, "What can you see in this feminine Solomon?" The answer is that this female Solomon is just like the dance of two camps.

Exodus 15:20 and 1 Samuel 18:6 tell us that dances among the Lord's people were a celebration of victory. When they defeated the enemy, they danced to celebrate their victory. This poetic expression shows us that this seeking one has victory all the time. There is never any defeat but always the celebration of victory.

Before I came to the church, I was with a group of believers who were seeking the Lord. They were good teachers of the Scriptures, but they were never victorious. Whenever I met with them, there was always a kind of sighing and confessing of their defeat. I never heard a praise of victory among them. That was surely not the Shulammite. But after I came into the church life, there was always the "Hallelujah! Amen! Jesus is Lord!" This was really the Shulammite in the dance of two camps to celebrate the victory.

When I was a young Christian, I was bothered by my temper. But now in the church life I realize that Christ is much bigger than my temper. I just say, "Hallelujah! Hallelujah! I'm in the corporate Shulammite, where there is always the victory!" Some people ask, "What is there to see in the local church?" We can only reply, "The dance of two camps!" This does not mean that I am encouraging you to dance. What I mean is that the real dance is the celebrating of our victory.

Hallelujah! In the local church we are always enjoying the victory over the enemy!

THE ALL-INCLUSIVE CHURCH

She is not only the city but also two armies. She is also the dawn, the moon, and the sun. The Lord has used so many figures in describing her. He has used the animals, the plants, the things on the earth, and the things in the sky. All these figures are used by the Lord to describe such a wonderful one. She must include all of us. We all must be like this. Some of us are still mares, some have doves' eyes, some are lilies, and some are little doves. Moreover, some are the pillars of smoke, the bed, the palanquin, and the crown. And, praise the Lord, some are the garden and the city. This is the local church! We are all-inclusively these figures under the Lord's transformation. Transformation can only be accomplished by enjoying the Lord Himself, step by step, in all the deeper experiences of His death and resurrection. Hallelujah! This is the real Song of Songs. The church is a real song to Christ, and Christ is the real Song of Songs to the church. Praise the Lord!

> Christ will make His seeking lover
> Pillar, couch, and palanquin,
> E'en a crown, His boast and glory;
> He will do it all! Amen!
>
> His beloved—how He loves her,
> So attractive, His delight.
> He is captivated wholly;
> She is comely in His sight.
>
> But there still remains a shadow;
> Christ is still not satisfied.
> He must have a growing garden
> To become His loving Bride!
>
> Paradise of pomegranates,
> Pleasant fruits, and henna flowers,
> Spikenard, saffron, myrrh, and aloes:
> His enjoyment now—not ours.

He has come into His garden,
  Gathered myrrh and spices there,
Eaten honeycomb and honey;
  Wine and milk He'll drink fore'er.

From the garden comes the city,
  All materials thus supplied;
God is satisfied completely,
  And the foe is terrified.

"Thou art fair, my love, as Tirzah,
  Comely as Jerusalem."
O Lord Jesus, Hallelujah,
  Thou wilt do it all! Amen!

(*Hymns,* #1161)

CHAPTER THIRTEEN

EQUIPPED TO WORK WITH THE LORD

Scripture Reading: S. S. 7:1, 4-8, 10-13

THE ETERNAL PURPOSE OF GOD

We have seen that the seeking one in the Song of Songs reached several attainments. First, she attained full satisfaction for herself. Then as a crown, she satisfied the Lord. Finally, she became a garden to satisfy the Lord and the Lord's people. In today's Christianity, nearly everyone would say that nothing else is needed. Our own need is taken care of, and we are taking care of others' needs. Seemingly, nothing else is required, but where is the fulfillment of God's purpose, the building up of the Body, the building up of the city?

Today nearly all Christians care only for their own needs, while some of the more improved Christians care for the needs of others. This might be considered the highest goal of today's Christian work. But all of this cannot reach God's goal, the building up of the Body. Almost no one cares for God's building. In these last ten years, many have begun to talk about the Body life and the Body ministry, but hardly anyone really understands what the Body is. The Body is a building; it is not a heaping up of materials.

Regardless of how much we undertake for our own satisfaction and how much we help others to be satisfied, we can only reach so far. God's purpose still is not fulfilled. This is why, after all the attainments of the seeking one, yet another step remains: that is, to care for God's eternal purpose, the building up of the Body, which is the building up of the city. It is not simply a matter of our being satisfied or of satisfying others but of the completing of the eternal purpose of God.

TWO ASPECTS OF THE LORD'S SUFFERING

How could the building up of the Body be accomplished? With the Lord's suffering, there are two aspects. One is for the accomplishment of redemption. The Lord Jesus suffered on the cross to accomplish redemption for us. This has been easily seen by all Christians. But there is another aspect of the Lord's suffering: His suffering for the formation and the building up of the Body. Most Christians today are completely ignorant regarding this very important aspect of the Lord's suffering. This is why Paul in Colossians 1:24 says, "I now rejoice in my sufferings on your behalf and fill up on my part that which is lacking of the afflictions of Christ in my flesh for His Body, which is the church." Paul says that he filled up the lack of the sufferings of Christ. The Lord's suffering for redemption has no lack. To say that would be heresy. For redemption, the Lord's suffering has been completed and is altogether sufficient. But His suffering for the producing, forming, and building up of the Body has a big lack. This is why Paul tells us that his suffering was a filling up of the lack of the Lord's suffering. We cannot suffer for the accomplishment of redemption, but we all must suffer for the building up of the Body.

SUFFERINGS FROM THE RELIGIOUS WORLD

If you are one who is simply seeking spirituality for your personal satisfaction, you will not suffer much. Rather, all the people of God will appreciate you and speak well of you because you are seeking spirituality. If you would go further to meet the need of others, you would be even more admired. All the religious people would never give you any trouble. But once you begin to see the need for the building up of the Body and to give yourself to this, you will suffer. Most of the suffering will not come from the world but from Christianity.

The Lord Jesus suffered for the producing of the Body, not from the Gentile world but from the Jewish religious world. Paul and the other apostles suffered very little from the

Gentiles, but they suffered very much from the Jewish religion and even to some extent from the Christian religion. Philippians 1 shows us that even some Christian preachers persecuted him. That was simply because Paul was for the building up of the Body.

Today it is exactly the same. If we would seek just to be spiritual and to care for others, not seeking to care for the Body, all Christianity would be happy with us. They would welcome us, invite us, and make a great name for us. We could become a famous preacher, pastor, or missionary. But once we see the vision of the Body and forget about all our individual seeking and caring for others in order to build up the Body, all Christianity will rise up against us. We must suffer to fill up what is lacking of the suffering of Christ for His Body's sake.

Even after the seeking one in the Song of Songs has reached the fourth attainment of being a garden, the Body still has not been attended to. There has been no building up of the city. She needs a further step to fulfill God's eternal purpose of building up the Body. If we would take this further step, surely we must share in the sufferings of Christ. This is why the apostle Paul used the term *the fellowship of His sufferings* in Philippians 3:10. We must share and participate in His sufferings, not for redemption, for that has already been accomplished, but for the building up of the Body, which has not yet been fully accomplished. We all must participate in the fellowship of His sufferings so that we may be conformed to His death for His Body's sake.

Christianity will not condemn us for our personal spirituality. They will not condemn us for our preaching the gospel to others and helping others to know the Lord. None of this would offend them. But when we go on to care for the ground of the church for the building up of the Body, they will be thoroughly offended. Just this one phrase, *one city, one church,* offends them all and will stir up all Christianity to oppose us. They would say, "What? Are you the church and we are not?" But what can we do? Can we only care for our personal spirituality, go to the mission field, set up a seminary to teach others, or teach some Bible study classes? What shall we do? If we would care for the Body, all our dear friends will become our enemies. They will do this not because we are heretical or because we are wrong in seeking spirituality and preaching the gospel. They will do it simply because we are for the building up of the one, unique Body.

THE CONSUMMATE ATTAINMENT

Finally, in the consummate attainment, the Lord likened the seeking one to six things: the city, the army, the dawn, the moon, the sun, and the dance of two camps. Now she is full of light, and there are no more shadows. Her day has fully dawned. She is a builded city for the Lord and a strong army to the enemy. She even appears as the dawn, the moon, and the sun, as well as celebrating the victory by the dance of two camps. She has really reached the final attainment.

QUALIFICATIONS FOR THE LORD'S WORK

Now we come to the Lord's final appraisal of the seeking one. Since she has reached the consummate attainment, she is now ready to work for the Lord. It is not a work *for* the Lord but a work *with* the Lord. She is now fully equipped and fully qualified to care for the Lord's work. This brings the Lord's last appraisal concerning her. All the aspects of this appraisal are related to her qualifications for the Lord's work.

HER FOOTSTEPS

The Lord first of all mentions something about her footsteps: "How beautiful are your footsteps in sandals, / O prince's daughter!" (S. S. 7:1). *Footsteps* indicates action that has already taken place. It is not a matter of the beauty of her feet but of her footsteps. This is the beauty of her action and her move. Her move is not with bare feet but with shoes! From Ephesians 6 we see that the shoes signify the preaching of the full gospel, including the preaching of the church life. The shoes not only give beauty to the feet but also keep the feet from the defilement of the earth. If we put our bare feet on the earth, they will become dirty. But if we have shoes on our feet, our feet are covered, protected, and separated from the earth, though they are so near to the earth. Hence, wherever we go—to the office, the factory, the school, or the store—we must wear our gospel shoes. The preaching of the gospel will protect us and keep us from becoming defiled through contact with the earth. When we arrive at a new job, go to a new school, or move to a new location, we must immediately let the people around us know that we wear the shoes of the gospel. If from the first day we tell them that they need Jesus, not one of them will ask us to go to the movies the next day. The shoes of the gospel will separate us from this world. The preaching of the full gospel always leaves a footstep that is beautiful in the eyes of the Lord.

THIGHS LIKE JEWELS

The second thing that the Lord mentions are the jewels: "Your rounded thighs are like jewels, / The work of the hands of a skilled artist" (S. S. 7:1). Jewels are precious gems that have been transformed. They were not originally in that state. This shows that she has been transformed by the skilled artist who is God Himself. Her thighs like jewels represent her standing power and stability. Without stability, we are not qualified to touch the work of the Lord. If we are going to work with the Lord, we need the stability of transformation.

NECK AS A TOWER OF IVORY

Then the Lord mentions her neck again: "Your neck is like a tower of ivory" (v. 4). In chapter 4 her neck was depicted as the tower of David, but here it is described as a tower of ivory. The tower of David was for fighting, but the tower of ivory means that her neck is full of resurrection life. Ivory in typology signifies the Lord's resurrection life. Now her neck is not only full of submission for fighting the spiritual warfare, but it is also full of the resurrection life. Her neck is a tower ministering life in resurrection.

EYES LIKE POOLS

Next, the Lord speaks of her eyes: "Your eyes, like the pools in Heshbon / By the gate of Bath-rabbim" (7:4). In chapter 1 her eyes were likened to doves' eyes, but now her eyes are likened to pools. We know that doves' eyes are very small,

but pools are much larger and have a much broader scope.
How much area can the doves' eyes cover compared with pools?
Now she has two large eyes, as big as pools. Such an enlarged
vision is really wonderful! The doves' eyes are spiritual, but
the eyes like pools are enlarged and broadened to cover the
whole universe.

Some seemingly spiritual people have the eyes of an ant.
Their eyes are even smaller than the eyes of a dove. They
cannot see anything except their work, their mission field,
their little group, their "church." But this seeking one can
now see the whole universe. There is no limitation to her
sight. We all need such a broadened vision. Her sight has
been enlarged to the size of pools. This is really meaningful.
Furthermore, these two pools are located by the gate. A gate
is for coming in and going out. This is the communication of
fellowship. If our eyes are as small as the ant's, it is really difficult for us to have fellowship with anyone. Our fellowship
depends upon our broadened sight.

Another matter concerning the pools is that they always
give some reflection. There is light in her sight. To care for
the Lord's work we need such a broadened sight full of light.
Otherwise, we are either short-sighted, narrow-sighted, or
even blind. We must become so enlarged in our vision that we
can see the whole universe. We not only care for the Lord's
work where we are, but we also care for the Lord's interests
in the whole universe.

NOSE AS THE TOWER OF LEBANON

Following the eyes, the Lord appraises her nose: "Your
nose is like the tower of Lebanon, / Which faces Damascus"
(v. 4). The Lord has never mentioned anything about her nose
until now. Her nose is like the tower of Lebanon. We know
that a tower is something elevated, and *Lebanon* means
ascension. Therefore, her nose is elevated by the Lord's ascension. The function of a nose is to smell. There are many things
that we cannot see, touch, or hear, but we can smell them.
The one who works with the Lord cannot be cheated. He does
not care for what you say; he cares for how you smell. He
does not care for things according to the outward appearance;

he cares for the inward scent. You may tell him that everything is fine, but immediately he senses something wrong, something not genuine, and something not in harmony with the Lord. Perhaps he could not say exactly what is wrong, but he knows that something is indeed wrong, because he has a nose like a tower. This is the safeguard of the Lord's work. It is really difficult to cheat one who has reached such an attainment. You may tell the truth, or you may tell him a lie. It makes no difference; it is still the same. It is not a matter of outward appearance but a matter of smell. For the safeguard of the Lord's work, we need such a nose like the tower of Lebanon.

FLOWING LOCKS LIKE PURPLE

Then the Lord comes again to her hair: "Your head upon you is like Carmel, / And the locks of your head like purple. / The king is fettered by your tresses" (v. 5). This time the Lord does not use the word *hair*. It is not the natural hair but the locks. A lock is a bundle of hair that has been dealt with, plaited and bound together. As we have already seen, this signifies her submission. Her will is fully dealt with, fully bound, and fully submitted to the Lord. With the locks are the beautiful tresses. It is the beauty of the tresses that captures the Lord. The king is fettered by her tresses. The Lord has become a captive to her submission. Her submission is so high, with the color of purple, that it brings in the Lord's kingship and authority.

In today's Christianity, you simply cannot see the Lord's headship, kingship, and authority. But, if we mean business with the Lord, we will have the color of purple in our submission to the Lord. The Lord's kingship is revealed in this way. It is the beauty of her submission that captures the Lord! The beauty of her submission "fetters" the king. The king was put in fetters by her submission. This is the real qualification for working with the Lord. If our natural life has not been subdued, if our hair has never been dealt with to be plaited and bound, then we are not qualified to touch the Lord's work. Spontaneously, there will be some amount of rebellion to the Lord. But with this one there is the submission to the uttermost, and the beauty of her submission holds the Lord as a captive. Marvelous!

HER BREASTS AS CLUSTERS OF GRAPES

The Lord goes on to mention something about her breasts: "This your stature is like a palm tree, / And your breasts are like the clusters" (v. 7). In chapter 4 her breasts were likened to fawns that were feeding. This meant that her faith and love were working to take something in for her own nourishment. But now her breasts have become clusters of grapes, not for her nourishment but for others. She is so full of life that she does not care much for her own needs. She mainly cares for others' needs. Eventually, she has a stature that is likened to a palm tree. This is the same as that which is mentioned in Ephesians 4:13. She has the measure of the stature of the fullness of Christ. She not only has all the other aspects, but she has also a full stature.

Now she is fully qualified to take care of the work of the Lord. In Song of Songs 4 it was the Lord who said to her, "Come with me." But now it is she who initiates the move with the Lord: "Come, my beloved, let us go forth into the fields; / Let us lodge in the villages. / Let us rise up early for the vineyards; / Let us see if the vine has budded, / If the blossom is open, / If the pomegranates are in bloom; / There will I give you my love" (S. S. 7:11-12). She initiates the work, and the Lord follows. The fields are the world in a general way, the villages are the local churches, and all the gardens are the different saints.

The problem is that we are all for our own places. We may all be for Jerusalem, but Judah is for Judah, and Benjamin is still for Benjamin. But let us go forth into the fields and lodge in the villages and look at all the gardens. We should not be shortsighted but have a broadened vision. We should be for all the churches in all the world. Hallelujah for all the churches throughout the world! Let us go forth into the fields and lodge in all the villages and visit all the gardens.

CHAPTER FOURTEEN

TRANSFIGURED TO MEET THE LORD

Scripture Reading: S. S. 8:1, 5-10, 13-14; Rom. 8:21-23; 2 Cor. 11:2; Deut. 4:24

A WIDER SIGHT

In the last chapter we saw how the seeking one took the initiative to work with the Lord. First, she asked the Lord to go with her into the fields. Then, she asked the Lord to go with her to lodge in the villages.

Again, she asked the Lord to go with her to visit the vineyards to see all the blooming and budding plants. She worked not only by taking the initiative but also, in type, by covering the whole earth with all the local churches. To go into the fields means to go to the earth. To lodge in all the villages means to lodge in all the local churches. To care for the budding and blooming plants is to care for all the individual believers.

If we are really qualified to work in the Lord and with the Lord, our scope and our sight will be widely broadened. We will never have the ant's eyes or even the doves' eyes anymore. Our eyes will be like pools with a broadened scope of the Lord's work. We will no longer simply care for the Lord's work where we are but will have a wider vision to cover all His work. Let us go into the fields. Let us lodge in all the villages, and let us visit every vineyard to see how the buds come forth. We need a heart that covers all the interests of the Lord in the entire earth.

THE LAST STEP

Though chapter 7 shows one who seems so qualified to work

together with the Lord, there is still a further need. No matter
how mature the seeking one has become, she still is in the old
creation; she still lives in the flesh. She is not absolutely the
same as the Lord. Hence, there is the need of the redemption
of the body, the last step of the experience of the Christian
life. We must be fully transfigured to the image of Christ even
in our body. Her spirit has been regenerated, and her soul has
been fully transformed, but her body is not the same as the
Lord's. There is still some element of weakness that others
could despise. No matter how much maturity she has in her
spirit and soul, she still lacks something in her body. She
needs to be transfigured.

THE RAPTURE BEING A PROCESS

Most Christians today have a strange concept concerning
the rapture. They think that it will come upon us as an accident. But the rapture is a process. We must be processed into
the rapture. In Revelation 14 there are the firstfruits and
then the harvest. This shows us that the rapture has something to do with maturity or ripeness. The rapture cannot
come suddenly. It is the final step of a process. It is just like a
crop in the field; it cannot be ripe all at once. The ripening is
a process by growth. The crop continues to grow, and as it
grows, it becomes ripe. The ripening stage does not come as an
accident, but is the final consummation of the process.

In Revelation 3:3 the Lord comes as a thief in the night.
We know that a thief does not steal worthless things. He only
takes the treasures. As long as we are untransformed, we can
be assured that the Thief will never come to visit us. The
Lord Jesus will not come as a gentleman to any of His people;
He will come as a thief to steal the precious things; He will
come as the Bridegroom to take the bride. A bride cannot be
produced overnight. The last chapter of the Song of Songs
mentions a little sister who has not yet grown up. Her faith
and her love have not been expressed. Surely, she could not be
a bride. She needs to grow unto maturity so that she may
be ripened for the Lord's coming.

THE EXPECTATION OF TRANSFIGURATION

Chapter 8 of the Song of Songs reveals this final stage of our Christian experience. The seeking one expresses it in this way: "Oh that you were like a brother to me" (v. 1). This means that she expects the Lord to become the same as she is. Of course, some may argue that the New Testament says that we will be the same as the Lord. But to say that one day we will be like Jesus is not so deep as to say that one day Jesus will be like us. But whether we are like Him or He is like us, we will be the same. The Lord Jesus will be the same as we are! But, of course, He will not be the same as we are today. He will be the same as we shall be when we are fully transfigured.

Some day we will be able to tell all the world to look at us and to look at Jesus. He has the human nature, and we do too. He has the divine nature, and we do too. He is so glorious, and we are so shining. We have His nature, and He has ours. We are like Him, and He is like us. "Oh that you were like a brother to me." This is a poetic expression of the expectation of the seeking one to be transfigured. One day she will be transfigured to His likeness, and He will be the same as she is. He will be her real brother, with the same nature, with the same life, and from the same source.

OUTSIDE OF THE BODY

Then she says something that is very meaningful: "If I found you outside, I would kiss you, / And none would despise me" (v. 1). To find you "outside" means outside of this body. Now we are still under the bondage of the old creation. According to Romans 8:21-23, the whole creation is groaning under slavery. Even those who have the Spirit as a foretaste are groaning for the release of this body. How we long to find the Lord outside. Even while we are fellowshipping with the Lord in our spirit, we are still in this troublesome flesh. We may say that we are sitting in the heavenlies, but we are still in the flesh. How much we long to be outside! Today we are meeting the Lord in the flesh, but we expect one day to meet Him outside of the flesh. Then we will kiss Him.

To find the Lord outside is the expectation of such a mature one in the Lord as the seeking one has now become. We can be assured that when we are as mature as she is in chapter 8 of Song of Songs, we will have no other expectation. The only expectation we will have is that we and the Lord will be exactly the same. Then, no one can despise us because of this body.

In our old nature, in our flesh, in this body, there is a real shortage. In my whole Christian life, I have never seen anyone who had no shortage for others to despise. "Oh that you were like a brother to me,... / If I found you outside, I would kiss you, / And none would despise me." All the factors that cause others to despise us will be swallowed up by our transfiguration. Today, in our flesh, there is a shortage in our natural makeup, no matter who we are. But one day this lack will be swallowed up. The transfiguration of life in our body will take care of all our shortage. Hallelujah!

GOING OUT OF THE WORLD WITH JESUS

At this point, someone asks again about the seeking one coming up from the wilderness. "Who is this who comes up from the wilderness, / Leaning on her beloved?" (v. 5). By this, we see that there are two wildernesses. We have seen, in chapter 3, the wilderness of our will. Here in chapter 8, we have the physical wilderness of the world. All the seeking Christians are going out of this world. I do not believe that anyone who is really seeking the Lord senses that he is a settler on the earth. We are not settlers in this world; we are pilgrims passing through.

No matter how long we live in Los Angeles, we are passing through Los Angeles. This earth to us is just a wilderness, and we are passing through. Here the seeking one is going out of the wilderness leaning on the Lord Jesus. In chapter 3 she was going out of that psychological wilderness as a pillar by herself. But now she is going out of the physical wilderness leaning on the Lord Jesus. This poetry depicts that as she is going out, she is one with the Lord Jesus.

We know that while we are waiting for the rapture, we are waiting for His coming. But this verse shows us that the Lord is not coming but going out with her. While she is going out of the world, she is leaning on the Lord. This clearly means that the Lord is going out of this world with her. We can well ask, "Is the Lord coming or going?" This is really difficult for our mind to comprehend.

We are waiting for His coming, yet He is going out with us. I can tell you that if He is not going out with us, we can never be waiting properly for His coming. If we would be one who is sincerely waiting for His coming, surely we need Him to go with us. He goes with us to meet Himself. He goes with us for His coming back.

We need not ask how this will happen. We know by our experience. While we are waiting for His coming, we are not going out of this world by ourselves. If we are, we will never go out! If, on the other hand, we are those who are really waiting for His coming, we will deeply sense that we are going out of this world leaning on Him. "O Lord Jesus, day by day I am going out with You, and You are going out with me for Your coming back." It may not appeal logically to our mind, but it is a fact.

The Lord Jesus is a wonderful person. He is going out with us, yet He is also coming. He told Nicodemus that while He was on the earth, He was still in heaven (John 3:13). He came from heaven, and then He was on the earth; yet, while He was on earth, He was still in heaven. All those who are really waiting for His coming are one with Him. Therefore, they are going out of this world, not by themselves but by Him. As we are going with Him, we realize that the "going-out" strength is not ours. We do not have the strength to go out. The going-out strength is simply Jesus. We lean on Him, and in a sense He bears us.

A SINNER SAVED BY GRACE

When the question is asked concerning the one going out of the wilderness, the Lord Jesus answers: "Who is this who comes up from the wilderness, / Leaning on her beloved? / I awakened you under the apple tree: / There your mother was in labor with you; / There she was in labor and brought you forth" (S. S. 8:5). The Lord answers that she is the one He awakened under the apple tree. We know from chapter 2 that the apple tree is the lovely and nourishing Christ. It was there that He regenerated her.

Who is this one? This one is simply a sinner, regenerated by God's grace in Christ. We should never consider that we are so high or wonderful. We must always realize that regardless of how mature we are, we are simply saved sinners. We are just under the lovely and nourishing Christ, regenerated by the grace and life of God. We should never forget what we were in the past. Before regeneration we were a fallen, corrupted, and deadened sinner. But one day God put us under the apple tree; He put us under the nourishing Christ and regenerated us.

No matter what position we may have in the church or how mature we are, we should never boast of it. Rather, we should always remember what we were. Our estate is still just a sinner saved by grace; this is all we are. For such an impression to be given in chapter 8 is very meaningful. If it had been given in chapter 1, it would not have been so significant. But here at the very consummation of her Christian life, the Lord reminds her that even now she is nothing. She is just a sinner saved by the grace of Christ. This is the answer the Lord gives concerning the seeking one.

LOVE AS STRONG AS DEATH

Following the Lord's answer, the seeking one prays a prayer. I do believe that none of us have ever heard such a prayer. "Set me as a seal on your heart, / As a seal on your arm; / For love is as strong as death, / Jealousy is as cruel as Sheol" (v. 6). We know that the heart signifies love, and the arm signifies power and strength. Therefore, this prayer indicates that she does not have any confidence in herself. She trusts in the Lord's loving heart and the Lord's mighty arm. She is praying in this way, "O Lord, keep me in Your loving heart, and preserve me by Your mighty arm. I have no trust in myself. Even though I am so matured, yet I am still in this flesh while I am going out of this world. Without Your keeping power and Your preserving love, I still may fall. So, Lord, keep me as a seal on Your heart and on Your arm."

This prayer indicates that she still realizes she is not trustworthy. She has no trust in herself. What a prayer this is! She is such a mature one, and yet she does not have any self-confidence. Her trust is fully in the Lord's love and might.

In her prayer, the seeking one says that the love of the Lord is as strong as death. Most Christians do not like to use a negative term to illustrate something of the Lord, as the Bible does here. If we had written the Bible, we would never have used the term *thief* to describe the Lord when He comes back. Not only good things but also some negative things illustrate the Lord Jesus. How negative death is! Yet there is nothing that describes the strength of the Lord's love as death does. Death is the strongest power in the universe, outside of God. When death visits a person, nothing can reject it. We cannot tell death that we are too busy and to wait for another three years. Praise the Lord, His love is as strong as death! When the love of the Lord touches us, we cannot say that we are too busy. His love will simply capture us! All the seekers of the Lord Jesus have been captured by His love. It is as strong as death.

JEALOUSY AS CRUEL AS SHEOL

Then she says that the Lord's jealousy is as cruel as Sheol. *Sheol* is the Hebrew equivalent of the Greek word *Hades,* where the dead are kept. Sheol is not the consummation of hell. The consummation of hell will be the lake of fire. But before that consummation, there is a place in this universe called Sheol that holds the dead. Nothing is as cruel as Sheol; it receives the dead without mercy. Though you love your dear wife, if Sheol comes to take her away from you, it has no mercy; it is so cruel. This describes the jealousy of our God. He is not only a loving God but also a jealous God. Deuteronomy 4:24 says, "Jehovah your God is a consuming fire, a jealous God."

This means that we have no trust in ourselves or in what we can be. Therefore, we ask the Lord to put us as a seal on His heart and on His arm. We put our trust in His love and strength, for His love is as strong as death and very jealous.

He would not allow our loved ones or anything else to keep us from Him. His jealousy is as Sheol. We should never trust in our love; our love is not trustworthy, and our love is not strong. Our love is always merciful and not so jealous. If we depend upon our love, two tears from our wife will turn us aside. But the love of Jesus has a terrible jealousy. He does not care, it seems, for the wife's tears or the husband's sympathy. The more the tears, the more He will take away her husband for Himself. He is jealous for Himself. He is a jealous God.

Then the prayer of the seeking one continues in this way: "Jealousy is as cruel as Sheol; / Its flashes are the flashes of fire, / A flame of Jehovah" (S. S. 8:6). With this love and with this jealousy is a flashing fire. We have already seen that God is not only a jealous God but also a consuming God. "Jehovah your God is a consuming fire." These two go together: the consuming God and the jealous God, the consuming fire and the jealousy.

Chapter 8 of the Song of Songs reminds us that even when we become so matured, we are only sinners saved by grace. We should never trust in ourselves, but put our trust in the jealous love of the Lord. Then we will be fully kept and preserved. We will never be carried away from the Lord. Otherwise, no matter how strong we are, we could be stolen away from the Lord by other things.

FROM FEEDING TO BUILDING

At this point in chapter 8, it seems that the Lord and the seeking one have fellowship together. "We have a little sister, / And she has no breasts: / What shall we do for our sister / On the day when she is spoken for? / If she is a wall, / We will build on her a battlement of silver; / And if she is a door, / We will enclose her with boards of cedar" (vv. 8-9). We have seen that in this book the two breasts are always symbols of faith and love. This means that here is a younger Christian whose faith and love have not yet matured. What shall we do with her?

In all the previous chapters, the most the seeking one did was to feed others, giving them something to eat and to drink.

But in this chapter it is not simply a matter of feeding and nourishing but also a matter of building up. This chapter does not say what we should do with her if she is hungry or thirsty, but that if she is a wall, we will build upon her, or if she is a door, we will build with her. Her words with the Lord have gone on from the feeding and nourishing aspect to the building aspect. This is a real improvement.

What does it mean to be a wall? This means a separation from the world unto God. It means a separation between the holy things and the unholy things. If she is a wall, we will build on her a battlement of silver. This means that something is built up with the Lord's redemption. A battlement refers to the high towers on the walls used for fighting. An ordinary wall has no battlement, and therefore is not useful for warfare. This means that if this younger Christian is separated from the world unto the Lord, we will build upon her a tower for battle with all the aspects of Christ's redemption. We will build upon her item after item, aspect after aspect of the Lord's redemption so that she may fight the battle. Then she will not only be a wall but a wall with a battlement.

The seeking one knows how to build this younger Christian not only if she is a wall but also if she is a door. A door in the Bible mainly signifies the experience of coming into the Lord's grace or coming into God Himself. Hence, if this younger Christian is a door through whom people may enter into the grace of God or God Himself, she must be built up with boards of cedar. Cedar, in typology, indicates the resurrected, ascended, glorified, and honored humanity of Jesus. If this young Christian is a door, she needs to be built up with such a humanity.

Now the seeking one knows not only how to nourish and feed others but also how to build them up. Furthermore, she knows what to build upon each person. She is unlike today's Christians, who try to help others but do not know whether the person they are helping is a wall or a door. All they know how to do is give them lectures, sermons, and Bible studies. The Lord's recovery, on the other hand, requires some experienced ones who know the Lord's building and who know how to build up others with proper materials. The wall needs a battlement, and the door requires boards of cedar. This is not merely a doctrine. This is the need among us in the Lord's recovery. Therefore, we must pray, "Lord, if I am a wall, build a battlement upon me. If I am a door, enclose me with the boards of cedar. How I need Your full redemption to equip me and Your all-inclusive humanity to enclose me."

COMING UPON THE MOUNTAINS OF SPICES

The last point in this book is in the very last verse: "Make haste, my beloved, / And be like a gazelle or a young hart / Upon the mountains of spices" (v. 14). As we have mentioned, this book is an extract of the entire Bible. It is a condensation of the Bible in eight short chapters. At the end of the Bible the Lord says, "I come quickly" (Rev. 22:20). To make haste means to come quickly. "Make haste, my beloved" means "Come quickly, Lord Jesus." The Lord is coming upon the mountains of spices. This is quite meaningful, for we have seen that in the Song of Songs the spices are the different aspects of the Lord Jesus experienced by us and even grown out from us. Soon, all our experiences of the Lord will be piled up like mountains. Then the Lord Jesus will come to meet us there. This will bring in the kingdom, and the kingdom will be composed of mountains of spices.

CHAPTER FIFTEEN

LIVING STONES FOR THE BUILDING

Scripture Reading: John 1:42; Matt. 16:16-18; 1 Cor. 3:9-13; 1 Pet. 2:5; Eph. 2:22; Rev. 21:18-19a, 14

The Lord's recovery is the recovery of life and building. In these chapters we have been considering life and building in the Song of Songs. We are not for the study of a book. We are for God's goal and purpose, which is life and building. In other Christian writings, it is difficult to find one book that puts these two words together. Have you ever read such a term, *life and building*? We may have heard the word *life* in Christianity, but we have rarely heard the word *building*. And we have never heard these two words together, *life and building*. Yet the central point of the Lord's recovery is life and building.

THE ENEMY'S DISTRACTIONS

Satan is so subtle. He has distracted nearly all the Lord's children from God's purpose through many good, scriptural, and spiritual things. Although there is nothing wrong with prophecy, many have been distracted by it. Others have been distracted by many other good subjects. The Bible is an all-inclusive book. Many things are in the Bible, but they are not the main goal of the Bible. The main goal of the Bible is life and building. Nearly all the sound, scriptural subjects have been utilized by the enemy to distract the Lord's children from life and building. Satan is happy if we spend all our time on so many scriptural things, as long as we do not see the building. As long as we do not care for the building, and as long as God's eternal goal cannot be accomplished, Satan would be happy.

Many good teachings, which on the one hand are helpful, on the other hand are distracting. Good, spiritual, and scriptural helps can become a frustration to us. Any point of spirituality can become our distraction. As long as we are content with what we have, we are frustrated and distracted. It may be something genuinely of God, yet it becomes a distraction from God's goal and purpose.

MISSING GOD'S PURPOSE

Many of us realize that the Catholic Church is quite devilish and even demonic. But we must admit that thousands of heathen have been brought to the Lord by the Catholic Church. Many devoted people are Catholics, spending all their time in prayer. But, though many have received help from the Catholic Church, they have been fully distracted from God's eternal purpose. Not one of them cares for God's eternal purpose. All have been distracted and frustrated.

Other Christians are also distracted by desiring to be spiritual, powerful, holy, and many other things. No doubt these are all good, but they are not God's purpose. God's purpose is not in our being powerful, holy, or spiritual. These very things have distracted many Christians from the central point of God's purpose.

PREDESTINED TO BE STONES

The central point of God's purpose is that you and I were predestined to be stones for His building. God has no intention that we be merely spiritual. God's intention is that we be stones for building. We are not to be stones for any kind of exhibition but for God's building.

Christians today talk much about the four Gospels. They admire the miracles done by the Lord and all His teachings, but not many have ever noticed this verse in John's Gospel: "He led him to Jesus. Looking at him, Jesus said, You are Simon, the son of John; you shall be called Cephas (which is interpreted, Peter)" (1:42). When Andrew brought his brother Simon to the Lord, the Lord changed his name to Cephas, which simply means "a stone." The first day he met the Lord Jesus, the Lord indicated that his destiny was to be a stone.

He did not say that Simon's destiny was to be anything else. The Lord's intention was not merely to save Peter but to make him a stone.

Two or three years later, the Lord reminded Peter again about his being a stone for His building. In Matthew 16:18, after Peter said that Jesus was the Christ, the Son of the living God, the Lord said, "I also say to you that you are Peter, and upon this rock I will build My church, and the gates of Hades shall not prevail against it." Based on the revelation of John 1:42, the Lord's word in Matthew 16 should be translated in this way: "I also say to you that you are *a stone,* and upon this rock I will build My church." When the Lord used the word *Peter,* He meant a stone. Peter recognized Him as the Son of the living God, and then the Lord reminded him that he was a stone for the building up of His church.

It is clear that Peter knew what the Lord meant, for later in his own writing, he wrote to the believers, "You yourselves also, as living stones, are being built up as a spiritual house into a holy priesthood to offer up spiritual sacrifices acceptable to God through Jesus Christ" (1 Pet. 2:5). We all have been predestined to be stones. Our destiny is to be living stones built up as the spiritual house of God. We must realize that this is not someone's opinion or concept but the central point in the Word of God.

MATERIALS FOR BUILDING

The apostle Paul also speaks about a building with stones. "We are God's fellow workers; you are God's cultivated land, God's building. According to the grace of God given to me, as a wise master builder I have laid a foundation, and another builds upon it. But let each man take heed how he builds upon it. For another foundation no one is able to lay besides that which is laid, which is Jesus Christ. But if anyone builds upon the foundation gold, silver, precious stones, wood, grass, stubble, the work of each will become manifest; for the day will declare it, because it is revealed by fire, and the fire itself will prove each one's work, of what sort it is" (1 Cor. 3:9-13).

Paul says that the apostles are God's fellow workers working with God. Their purpose is to build. And we are God's building. On one hand, we are the materials for the building, and on the other hand, we are the co-builders with God. This is why Paul says that we must all be careful with what material we build. We can build with gold, silver, and precious stones, or wood, grass, and stubble. There are two categories of materials. The first category is fireproof, whereas the second is the best material for burning. If we were to construct a building of gold, silver, and precious stones, the fire department would immediately approve it; it would be one hundred percent fireproof.

COVERED AND VEILED

In 1 Corinthians Paul tells us clearly that we are the building of God. We are not destined to be this or that. We are destined to be stones built up in God's house.

Before we came to the church life, we seldom heard of our being stones for the building. Most Christians completely miss God's central purpose. May the Lord have mercy upon us that we may see something deeper, higher, and richer. We should not care for wood, grass, and stubble. We are here to be precious stones for the building. For us to see this requires the Lord's mercy.

Paul says in 1 Corinthians 3 that he is the master builder who has laid the foundation, and that the Corinthians are the building as well as the co-builders. Therefore, they must be the proper building with the proper materials. The matter of building is so clear in this book, yet most Christians today will not see it. They can read this book many times, but they see nothing of the building. Instead, they pick up the negative things and argue for them. I have never met one Christian in Christianity who asked about the building in 1 Corinthians 3. It is because most of the Christians today have been distracted and veiled. Tongue-speaking, divine healing, and many other things have become layer upon layer of veils to them. Tongue-speaking is one layer; divine healing is another; even spirituality is another. We must get through all these layers! We should not care merely for spirituality; we should not care merely for being holy. We should care for God's building!

·

STONES, STONES, STONES

Many scriptural things have been used by the enemy to distract and to veil the Lord's children. We need the unveiling in order that we may see the light. Then our eyes will be enlarged to be like pools. Look at all these verses. John 1:42 has the word *stone*. Matthew 16:18 has *stone*. First Corinthians 3:12 has *stones*. First Peter 2:5 has *stones*. And Revelation 21:19 has *stone*. All we have in these verses are stones, stones, and more stones. Matthew is the first book of the New Testament, and Revelation is the last. From the beginning to the end of the New Testament, we see stones. It is a book of stones! The Lord Jesus mentions stones, Peter mentions stones, Paul mentions stones, and John mentions stones. Peter, Paul, and John are the main writers in the composition of the New Testament, and all their writings speak of stones for the building.

At the very beginning of the New Testament age, when Simon came to Jesus, the Lord immediately changed his name to Peter, which means "a stone." After Peter stayed with the Lord for two or three years, he recognized Him as the Christ, the Son of the living God. Then the Lord told him that there is also something else. "You are a stone," He said, "for the building up of My church." Then later Peter told the saints that they were all living stones to be built up as a spiritual house. Paul also spoke the same thing, and eventually the apostle John gave the conclusion to the whole New Testament and even to the entire Bible. He said that the wall of the New Jerusalem is jasper, a precious stone, and the foundations of the wall are adorned with every precious stone. So at the end of the entire Bible we see a building that has been built up with precious stones, with Peter as one of the twelve foundation stones, for the foundation stones bear the names of the twelve apostles.

This is not my teaching, message, or opinion. This is the Lord's recovery. It has been buried in the Bible for centuries, but now the Lord has been merciful to us and has removed the covering. Now we see that we are all stones to be built up for God's building. The enemy is so subtle. He does his best to make the situation foggy and cloudy. We must pray, "Lord, take away all the fog and the clouds. Grant us a clear sky to see Your eternal purpose." For the church to go on, we all need a clear sky without any fog or cloud.

A DEFINITE GOAL

Some may say that since the churches are all-inclusive, we need many things. Yes, the churches are all-inclusive but with a meaning and a definite goal. They should be just like the Bible—all-inclusive but having a definite goal. The Bible covers everything, but everything is not the goal. I could sacrifice my fingers or my toes, but I could never sacrifice my head! You can take away some of my fingers or some of my toes, and I can still live. But if you try to take away my head, I will die right away. If I lose my head, I lose my life. To remove some of my toes is comparatively insignificant, but I could never allow you to take off my head. This is why we can sacrifice some things, but life and building we can never sacrifice. This is the goal of the Bible.

THE LOCAL BUILDING

Ephesians 2:22 says, "In whom you also are being built together into a dwelling place of God in spirit," after verse 21 has said, "In whom all the building, being fitted together, is growing into a holy temple in the Lord." Using verse 21, some say that Ephesians is for the universal church, for it says that we all are built together spiritually, no matter where we are physically. You may be in London, I may be in Jerusalem, and another may be in New York, but we are all the building being fitted together. I do not contend with this, but we must also read verse 22. Paul says, "You also." He is speaking of the saints in that locality. The local saints must be built up together into a dwelling place of God in spirit. This is not the universal building; this is the local building.

Now we must speak practically. Perhaps we agree that our destiny is to be a stone for God's building. Then I would ask, "With whom are you built up in the locality where you are?" Do not say that you are built up with the apostle Paul. You need to be built up with the brothers in your place and with the saints with whom you serve. Surely the twelve apostles were built up, for they became the twelve layers of foundation stones for the New Jerusalem.

GOD'S CENTRAL GOAL

Our destiny is just to be stones for the building. Many Christians today have been asking why the Lord has not come back. It is because there is no building. He has no way to come back unless there is the building. In the Catholic Church, in the denominations, and in the free groups, there is absolutely no building. Among all the seeking Christians today, where is the building? We all have liberty to do something for the Lord. Many would ask, "What is wrong with doing something for the Lord? Why do I have to work together with you? You have the liberty to do something for the Lord, and I do too. You go your way, and I go mine. What is wrong with what I am doing?" There may be nothing wrong, but where is the building?

Others would say that they have the Lord's blessing in what they are doing. I do not deny this, but we have to realize that even the devilish Catholic Church has some of the Lord's blessing. The Lord is not so small. He is bigger than the universe. He would use any kind of way. You were saved in one way, but He has a thousand ways for people to be saved. Just because the Lord is so great does not justify us or mean that what we are doing is on His heart. To do what is on His heart is another thing. Thousands of pagans have been brought to the Lord through the devilish Catholic Church, yet we can hardly believe that the Catholic Church is on the Lord's heart. The Lord can use it but only to a small extent.

What the Lord is after today is someone to fulfill His purpose and to heed His goal, and by the Lord's mercy that is why we are here. We are here for the Lord's goal of life and building. So we should never be distracted by anything else. We must absolutely give ourselves to this one thing—life and building. I can assure you that this is what the Lord is seeking today. Our destiny is just for His building. The Scriptures show clearly that we need the growth and transformation in life for the building. The growth in life is for the building; the transformation in life is for the building.

I am so happy that in the past years I have seen the growth among the saints and also the building up. We need to check ourselves by the growth in life and the building up. There is no other way to fulfill the Lord's purpose, and this is why these are the main things in the Lord's recovery. Many things may be helpful, but they are not the central goal of God's purpose. The central goal of God's purpose in the Bible is life and building. May the Lord open our eyes so that we may see it.

Chapter Sixteen

THE DESTINATION OF BUILDING

Scripture Reading: 1 Pet. 2:2; 1 Cor. 1:10; 3:6; Eph. 4:2-3, 15-16; Phil. 2:2-3

The final need of the seeking one is the building up. We may be like a mare or so improved that we are like a dove or even a palanquin, but we still need to go on to be the city! The building up of the city should be our destination. Our Christian life must continually improve until it reaches the building. Christians today have many different goals. But in the Word we see clearly that the destination of our Christian life is simply the building. There is no need to wait until eternity to reach this destination. The Word tells us that we should reach it in this age, while we are still living in the flesh. If we would read all the Epistles again with the viewpoint of the building, we would see that they all are for this destination. They all point toward the goal of the building.

THE ORDER OF THE NEW TESTAMENT

Consider the arrangement of the books of the New Testament. They are arranged very much in order, just like our body. Our head is on top, and our feet are on the bottom. In the same way, the book of Revelation is at the end of the New Testament. It is indeed significant that the four Gospels are at the beginning, followed by the Acts and the Epistles. The book of Romans does not follow the four Gospels. It was clearly the work of the Holy Spirit that all the books were arranged in such a good sequence. The Gospels are at the beginning, followed by the Acts, the Epistles, and then Revelation.

Christ as such a wonderful person is first of all presented

in the four Gospels. These Gospels are simply a record and revelation of such a wonderful person. He is not only God but also man. He is not only life but also the way. He is not only the Savior but also the life-giving Spirit. He is the all-inclusive One. He is the Triune God; He is the Father, the Son, as well as the Spirit! He is everything! He is our God, our Creator, our Redeemer, our Savior, our Lord, our life-giving Spirit, our way, our life, our everything! Such a One is our humility, our patience, and our wisdom. He is revealed in a full record of four books.

After the revelation of this wonderful person, the book of Acts shows the spreading of such a person. He was spread to the north, the south, the east, and the west. He was brought to every direction and imparted into so many human beings.

Following the Acts, the Epistles tell us how this wonderful person can come into us so that we can be built up together. First Corinthians tells us how He is everything to us, and how we must become precious stones to be built up together as God's dwelling place. First Corinthians also shows us many distracting elements that cause Christians to be divided. This is why Paul told them, "I beseech you, brothers, through the name of our Lord Jesus Christ, that you all speak the same thing and that there be no divisions among you, but that you be attuned in the same mind and in the same opinion" (1:10). We need to be attuned in the same mind and the same opinion. Paul also says in Romans 15:6 that the whole Body needs to have one mind and one mouth. All these passages indicate the oneness in building up.

THE SUBSTANTIAL BUILDING

Hence, we see that all the books of the New Testament are arranged in a marvelous sequence. But this is not simply for the sake of appearance. It is for the building. I had been reading and studying the Bible for many years, yet I did not see anything about the building. Only in recent years have I begun to see such a central, solid, and substantial thing as the building in the Bible.

Now we can see that all the Epistles were written for this one purpose and destination. We all must reach this destination. How wonderful that we have received Christ and are enjoying Him as grace! But we must reach the destination, which is the building up. This is not something for the next age; it is for this age. And it is not something in the air, but solidly on the earth. By my experience, I can tell you that this is really substantial. It is so real, and it is so reachable. All the New Testament Epistles simply bring us to this one destination.

We all are familiar with the book of Revelation, the last book of the New Testament. At the beginning, it speaks of the lampstands, which are built up in different localities. The lampstand signifies the building up. In Ephesus there was one lampstand, and in Smyrna there was also one lampstand. In each one of the seven cities in Asia mentioned in the first chapter of Revelation, there was a lampstand. The lampstands are not for the next age. The Lord wants us all to be built up together as a lampstand in the locality where we are. Then the book of Revelation ends by speaking of a city that has been built up with precious stones. Hence, it is right to say that the Song of Songs is an extract of the whole Bible. The Song of Songs also has a city at the end, and this city is the bride of Solomon. The city at the end of Revelation is the bride of the Lamb (21:2). And like the Song of Songs, this city really looks like the dawn, the moon, and the sun. There is even no night there (Rev. 21:25).

The New Testament shows that all other things are passing away. Only one thing is increasing, and that is the building. The more we grow in life, the more so many other things will pass away. Perhaps today we still hold on to doctrinal toys, but if we grow in life, so many toys will disappear. When a man becomes as old as I am, he has no more interest in toys. By growing in life, the toys of doctrines and gifts simply pass away. Eventually, there is only one thing left—the building up.

THE PRACTICAL CHURCH LIFE

Up to the first part of the twentieth century the Lord used many different saints to recover numerous items for His recovery. Nearly all the items that needed to be recovered have been recovered. Now the Lord's intention is to put all the items of His recovery together to build up the local lampstands. The Lord's recovery today is simply the building up of the local lampstands, or in other words, the real practice of the church life. This is so practical. Nearly all the spiritual things have been recovered, and today the Lord is seeking the real practice of the church life. It is not simply some teaching, revelation, vision, theory, or principle of the Body that the Lord is seeking, but a real, solid practice of the church life. This is the real building up.

Many of us can testify that until we came to the practical church life, we were never satisfied. The day we came to the church, we realized we were home. We were home because the Lord in us was home. But simply to come to the church is not enough. We must be built up. At first the church life is so sweet to us, and we have a real honeymoon. But a honeymoon cannot last forever. Sooner or later we may begin to have some problems with the brothers and sisters. How good it was to get into the church life, but gradually, the dear ones become not so dear to us. We know that we should love them, but it is so hard to love them. This exposes our real need of building up.

If a group of brothers are living together in the brothers' house, it is so sweet at the beginning. Everyone quotes Psalm 133: "Behold, how good and how pleasant it is / For brothers to dwell in unity!" But after a while, dwelling together is not so sweet. Then what shall we do? At this point some leave. They simply cannot take it any longer. This is because they do not have the building up, and they do not want the building up.

THE MAIN LESSON

The main lesson I have learned in all these years is the building up. Many people are seeking to be holy and spiritual, but without being built up they are still short of the Lord's goal. Though some may be holy and spiritual, without the building they are still unable to fulfill God's consummate purpose. If holiness and spirituality are not for the building up of the local church, they are still short of God's purpose.

God's purpose is the building, and this can be proved by the end of Revelation. All God's work throughout the centuries and the generations is for the building up of the New Jerusalem. What comes forth at the end of the Bible is not a group of spiritual persons or holy people but a built-up city. This is all God cares for. He does not care merely for our being holy. He does not care merely for our being spiritual. The only thing He eventually cares for is the building. If you are not in the building, you are missing the mark.

In God's eyes, there is nothing in every locality but a lampstand. All the spiritual persons must lose their identity to be built up into the lampstand. All the lessons in the brothers' houses are for the building. All experiences are for the building. Anything that is not for the building is not of much worth. Even salvation is for the building. When Peter was brought to the Lord, he was given a new name indicating that he was to be a stone in God's building. The Lord saved Peter so that he could be built up in His church.

SHAMING THE ENEMY

By the Lord's mercy, we are not here simply to be Christians or to have good meetings. We are not here for anything but the building. God needs a building in Los Angeles, and He needs a building in your city. Nothing shames the enemy as much as the building. As long as we are built up together, the enemy is put to shame. The enemy has been boasting much to the Lord throughout the centuries concerning the divisive situation of Christianity. But I believe the Lord is telling him now, "Satan, wait for a little while and you will see a building in Los Angeles and in so many other cities!"

NOW BEING THE TIME

We must cooperate with the Lord by saying, "Lord, now is the time. You must shame Your enemy by building us up together." This will defeat the enemy. I have the full assurance that the Lord is going to do this. If we do not afford Him the opportunity to do it, He will find others who will. But the Lord will get His building and shame His enemy.

Revelation 19 tells us clearly that the Lamb will come as

the Bridegroom to take His bride, who has made herself ready. But without the building, where is the possibility of the Lord having such a bride? Is it in the Catholic Church? Is it in the denominations? Is it in the free groups or in the scattered so-called spiritual ones? Where is the bride being prepared? We should not care much for increase in numbers. Increase does not mean that much, but the building means everything. In the Lord's recovery we are only for the building.

I love the brothers in the churches in Texas. If you were to go visit them, you would see that they care for nothing but the building. In a sense, they are a real army with an impact. They do not have extensive Bible knowledge, and they do not know very much. They only know one thing: to be one. And they are one, praise the Lord!

We all must realize that the real impact which puts the enemy to shame is the building. The building is the impact. We all must pray, "Lord, I am through with so many things that I appreciated in the past. I want to leave all those things behind. Only one goal is before me, and that is Your building. I am not for anything that hinders, hurts, or damages Your building!"

We should not care merely for our holiness and spirituality. I do not mean that we should not pray or that we should not take the Word into us. What I mean is that everything we do must be for the building. Anything that distracts us from the building must be put aside. No matter how good or spiritual it seems to us, we must leave it if it is a frustration to God's building. If we take this attitude, we will have the Lord's rich presence, and we will experience the anointing with life and peace within. Then Satan will really be defeated and put under our feet. As long as we are in the building, there is no need to fight against him; he is defeated already. If, however, we are divided and scattered, Satan will get the glory.

EATING THE WORD

Now we must see some of the practical matters concerning the building. If we are really for God's building, the first thing we must do is eat the Lord in the Word all the time. I say this from my own experience, and it is confirmed by the experience of many others. To eat means to take something into you. It is not to learn about something but to digest and assimilate food. Day by day we must take the Lord Jesus into us. The best way to take the Lord in is to pray-read the Word or to pray Him in by calling on His name. I do not mean to pray in a way of asking the Lord to do something for you. The Lord already knows all our needs and will care for us. There is hardly any need to remind Him of these things. But we must spend more and more time to pray Him in. Then, practically speaking, in all our daily life we must learn to apply Him in many areas.

Praise the Lord that He is such a real person to us! He is not vain; He is real! He is not far away from us; He is within our spirit! So we must pray, "Lord Jesus, I take You in." He is a real person, and He is so substantial. This is why Peter says, "As newborn babes, long for the guileless milk of the word in order that by it you may grow unto salvation" (1 Pet. 2:2). What is the pure milk of the word? It is simply Jesus as the life-giving Spirit. He is in the word, and He even is the word. Then Paul says, "I planted, Apollos watered, but God caused the growth" (1 Cor. 3:6). The real growth is Jesus added into us. Paul planted Jesus into the Corinthians, and Apollos watered with the living water, which is also Jesus. Then God caused the growth, which is the increase, the addition of Jesus. In this way, Jesus is added into us bit by bit. This is not a matter of knowledge, doctrine, power, ability, or gifts. It is a matter of Jesus Himself being added into us all the time.

A METABOLIC CHANGE

If we mean business in taking Jesus into us in this way, we will experience a real change in life. We know that eating really changes people. The more we eat, the more we are changed. It is a metabolic change. When the new elements enter into us, they replace the old. During a period of one hundred twenty days, all our blood cells are replaced with new cells. If we were to keep the old cells for a period of time, we would die. Of course, such a thing is not possible physically, but I do believe that it is possible spiritually. If we still hold on to the old things, nothing will be replaced within us. We do need this metabolic change. When a new, nourishing element of Jesus gets into us, it carries away the old element and replaces it with something new. This is the transforming work of Jesus that results from taking Him into us. This kind of metabolic change regulates us but not in an outward way. It is an inward regulation through the replacing of the old with the new.

If some of us are living together as roommates, there will be many opportunities for this inward regulation and change to work. We may feel that a certain brother is quite undesirable, but if we would take some new element of Jesus into us, we would have a completely different feeling about that brother. We will begin to feel that we really need him for the building.

THE HUMANITY OF CHRIST

When I was a young Christian, I was taught the verses in Ephesians 4:2-3: "With all lowliness and meekness, with long-suffering, bearing one another in love, being diligent to keep the oneness of the Spirit in the uniting bond of peace." Lowliness, meekness, and long-suffering were really a suffering to me. The more I tried to be lowly, the more high-minded I was. And the more I tried to be meek, the more unyielding I was. I believe that we all have had these experiences of trying to be lowly, meek, and long-suffering. These are not vain words in the Bible; they are really meaningful, but we must realize that they are the expression of Christ. Lowliness really is not lowliness. Lowliness is Christ! As for meekness, it cannot be found in the whole universe outside of Christ. Meekness is Christ. Christ never meant for us to be meek. We must experience Christ as our meekness.

It is easy to understand these verses in Ephesians in a natural way—even a child can read and understand them. But these two verses are the most difficult verses for Christians to realize. The more we seek lowliness, the more lowliness flies away. Eventually, we simply will not believe that there is such a thing as lowliness in the whole universe. The Bible speaks about it, but we simply cannot find it. The Bible speaks also of long-suffering, which really means long endurance, but where is it? The more we attempt to endure, the shorter our endurance is. When we try to be patient, patience flies away. We come to the conclusion that the dictionaries are propagating lies. They explain what these things are, but there are no such things to be found.

Praise the Lord that by His grace we have begun to know a little bit about patience. Patience is just Christ! Long-suffering or long endurance, which some versions render as making allowances for others, is Christ. There is no such thing as making allowances for others without Christ. If we have the proper experience of Christ, we will understand what these verses mean. All the virtues of the proper humanity are just Christ Himself. Christ is our lowliness, and Christ is our meekness. Some may say that they are full of meekness, but their kind of meekness could only last for three or four hours. Then it will vanish away.

Philippians 2:2-3 says, "Make my joy full, that you think the same thing, having the same love, joined in soul, thinking the one thing, Doing nothing by way of selfish ambition nor by way of vainglory, but in lowliness of mind considering one another more excellent than yourselves." These verses sound so desirable that we might be tempted to fulfill them ourselves. But we must be clear that these verses do not describe any human virtue besides Christ. All these virtues are the attributes of the humanity of Jesus. His humanity is the summation of all human virtue. It is by His humanity that we are built up. We can never be built up by our own attributes or our own human virtues. We can only be built up by the experience of Christ as all these human virtues. Every item is a part of the expression of Christ and will last for eternity. The meekness that is Jesus can never be exhausted! The more we test it, the more it lasts. It can stand any kind of test. This is what we need for the building. All these virtues are simply the expression of our inner growth of Christ.

BUILT UP AND BUILT IN

When we eat Jesus, all the nourishing elements of His life

give us the metabolism that produces all kinds of expressions in our human conduct. This is especially true in the small things. By these experiences we are not only built up but also built in. If others try to pull us out of the church, they cannot do it. To pull us out they would have to pull out the whole church, for we are built in. I am burdened for those who are on the outskirts of the church life. If they are not built in by experiencing the humanity of Christ, Satan will tempt them to leave the church. But, praise the Lord, Christ is such a One whom we can experience! I can tell you that for the past forty years I have been solidly built in. There is such a real thing as the building up. Even if others were to kill me, they could not pull me out of the church life.

The longer we stay in the church life, the more our peculiarity is exposed. All the saints are peculiar. Without the church, we might consider ourselves quite normal, but after being in the church life for a time, we begin to realize that we are peculiar and even abnormal. We need the transformation that comes by eating. The more we are transformed, the more we can fit into the situation, and the more we can make allowances for others. Then we are really built in.

The Lord's recovery is just the building up, and by the Lord's mercy we are in it. This is a real shame to the enemy and a glory to the Lord! Nothing is so glorious to the Lord Jesus as the building. And this is why nothing satisfies us like the proper church life. How He is satisfied with the building! And how much we ourselves have been satisfied! When we are satisfied, it is a sign that He is satisfied. On the other hand, when we are not satisfied, He is not satisfied. Both we and the Lord can only be satisfied with the building. Praise the Lord! There is no other way. This is the only way to prepare for His coming back. The Lord is going to build up the church in many places to shame the enemy and prepare His bride. This is the Lord's building today, and many more are going to be built in. Although we do not care for numbers, I do believe that we will see a large number of good, solid ones added to the building. This is the Lord's recovery today. May the Lord grant us the sufficient grace for this purpose.

I love Thee, Jesus,
And Thy love to me
Draws me, ever to seek Thee
    And run after Thee,
Draws me, ever to seek Thee
    And run after Thee.
        Thou art beloved,
        Yea! Altogether lovely,
        The One in whom my heart delighteth.
        (Repeat last 3 lines of each verse)

Thy love, Lord Jesus,
Is sweeter than wine,
And Thy fragrance of ointments
    My heart doth entwine,
And Thy fragrance of ointments
    My heart doth entwine.
        A fount in gardens,
        A well of living waters,
        Which streams and flows from Lebanon's
            mountains.

O come Beloved,
On my garden blow,
That the odor of spices
    May break forth and flow,
That the odor of spices
    May break forth and flow.
        My spouse, My sister,
        I'm come into My garden
        To feast upon wine, milk, and honey.

Set me, Lord Jesus,
A seal on Thine heart,
Jealousy's cruel as Sheol,
    And love's strong as death
Jealousy's cruel as Sheol,
    And love's strong as death.
        Much water cannot
        Quench love, nor do floods drown it.
        All man could give for love is contemned.

(*Hymns,* #1154)

ABOUT THE AUTHOR

Witness Lee was born in 1905 in northern China and raised in a Christian family. At age 19 he was fully captured for Christ and immediately consecrated himself to preach the gospel for the rest of his life. Early in his service, he met Watchman Nee, a renowned preacher, teacher, and writer. Witness Lee labored together with Watchman Nee under his direction. In 1934 Watchman Nee entrusted Witness Lee with the responsibility for his publication operation, called the Shanghai Gospel Bookroom.

Prior to the Communist takeover in 1949, Witness Lee was sent by Watchman Nee and his other co-workers to Taiwan to ensure that the things delivered to them by the Lord would not be lost. Watchman Nee instructed Witness Lee to continue the former's publishing operation abroad as the Taiwan Gospel Bookroom, which has been publicly recognized as the publisher of Watchman Nee's works outside China. Witness Lee's work in Taiwan manifested the Lord's abundant blessing. From a mere 350 believers, newly fled from the mainland, the churches in Taiwan grew to 20,000 in five years.

In 1962 Witness Lee felt led of the Lord to come to the United States, and he began to minister in Los Angeles. During his 35 years of service in the U.S., he ministered in weekly meetings and weekend conferences, delivering several thousand spoken messages. Much of his speaking has since been published as over 400 titles. Many of these have been translated into over fourteen languages. He gave his last public conference in February 1997 at the age of 91.

He leaves behind a prolific presentation of the truth in the Bible. His major work, *Life-study of the Bible,* comprises over 25,000 pages of commentary on every book of the Bible from the perspective of the believers' enjoyment and experience of God's divine life in Christ through the Holy Spirit. Witness Lee was the chief editor of a new translation of the New Testament into Chinese called the Recovery Version and directed the translation of the same into English. The Recovery Version also appears in a number of other languages. He provided an extensive body of footnotes, outlines, and spiritual cross references. A radio broadcast of his messages can be heard on Christian radio stations in the United States. In 1965 Witness Lee founded Living Stream Ministry, a non-profit corporation, located in Anaheim, California, which officially presents his and Watchman Nee's ministry.

Witness Lee's ministry emphasizes the experience of Christ as life and the practical oneness of the believers as the Body of Christ. Stressing the importance of attending to both these matters, he led the churches under his care to grow in Christian life and function. He was unbending in his conviction that God's goal is not narrow sectarianism but the Body of Christ. In time, believers began to meet simply as the church in their localities in response to this conviction. In recent years a number of new churches have been raised up in Russia and in many European countries.

Other Books Published By
Living Stream Ministry

Titles by Witness Lee:

Abraham—Called by God	978-0-7363-0359-0
The Experience of Life	978-0-87083-417-2
The Knowledge of Life	978-0-87083-419-6
The Tree of Life	978-0-87083-300-7
The Economy of God	978-0-87083-415-8
The Divine Economy	978-0-87083-268-0
God's New Testament Economy	978-0-87083-199-7
The World Situation and God's Move	978-0-87083-092-1
Christ vs. Religion	978-0-87083-010-5
The All-inclusive Christ	978-0-87083-020-4
Gospel Outlines	978-0-87083-039-6
Character	978-0-87083-322-9
The Secret of Experiencing Christ	978-0-87083-227-7
The Life and Way for the Practice of the Church Life	978-0-87083-785-2
The Basic Revelation in the Holy Scriptures	978-0-87083-105-8
The Crucial Revelation of Life in the Scriptures	978-0-87083-372-4
The Spirit with Our Spirit	978-0-87083-798-2
Christ as the Reality	978-0-87083-047-1
The Central Line of the Divine Revelation	978-0-87083-960-3
The Full Knowledge of the Word of God	978-0-87083-289-5
Watchman Nee—A Seer of the Divine Revelation ...	978-0-87083-625-1

Titles by Watchman Nee:

How to Study the Bible	978-0-7363-0407-8
God's Overcomers	978-0-7363-0433-7
The New Covenant	978-0-7363-0088-9
The Spiritual Man • 3 volumes	978-0-7363-0269-2
Authority and Submission	978-0-7363-0185-5
The Overcoming Life	978-1-57593-817-2
The Glorious Church	978-0-87083-745-6
The Prayer Ministry of the Church	978-0-87083-860-6
The Breaking of the Outer Man and the Release ...	978-1-57593-955-1
The Mystery of Christ	978-1-57593-954-4
The God of Abraham, Isaac, and Jacob	978-0-87083-932-0
The Song of Songs	978-0-87083-872-9
The Gospel of God • 2 volumes	978-1-57593-953-7
The Normal Christian Church Life	978-0-87083-027-3
The Character of the Lord's Worker	978-1-57593-322-1
The Normal Christian Faith	978-0-87083-748-7
Watchman Nee's Testimony	978-0-87083-051-8

Available at
Christian bookstores, or contact Living Stream Ministry
2431 W. La Palma Ave. • Anaheim, CA 92801
1-800-549-5164 • www.livingstream.com